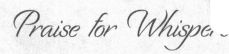

Praise for Whispers

"*Whispers from His Heart* is a devotional journal written to inspire, uplift, and encourage anyone that reads it. As you deal with everyday situations, allow it to speak to you as you experience God's goodness. It is certain to bring hope to your heart."

Ora Hart, Alabama Women's Discipleship Director
Church of God State Executive Offices

"Brenda has transcribed the loving words the Lord spoke to her in her latest book, *Whispers from His Heart*. These words will encourage, brighten, and lift you up no matter the depth of your circumstances. Take a journey into the whispers of the Lord."

Pastor Norm and Liz Hewitt
Real Church, Guntersville, AL

"Written in the style of Sarah Young's *Jesus Calling*, *Whispers* is a daily devotional that does exactly what the name suggests; it whispers aptly spoken words to the quiet place of your heart. Unlike other devotionals, *Whispers* does more than cite scripture references; it includes actual scripture, which helps prevent interruption during devotional time. Brenda W. Powell is a gifted artist. Her words are textured, like an ornate tapestry that causes you to pause and ponder the life of its Creator. *Whispers from His Heart* will provoke you to pursue God's presence, probe your heart, and prompt you to pray throughout your day."

Toya Poplar, speaker and author of *Stop Write There*

"*Whispers from His Heart* is not only encouraging but is genuine and exciting! Brenda invites you into her personal journal where God lovingly reinforces the truth that we can do nothing apart from Jesus. While in the hustle of life, this devotional reminds you to be still, to trust, and to remember you don't have to do it all because Christ already has! It is a must-have bedside book for any season of life and also a great gift to inspire a friend."

Ashley Smith, worship leader/songwriter
www.ashleysmithmusic.com

"My family and I have been tremendously blessed by Brenda's children's book series, *The Adventures of Sugarman the Pony.* I know that your life will be charged, challenged, and changed as you read this *Whispers* devotional. May you experience the heart of the Father, feel the love of the Savior, and sense the gentle touch of the Holy Spirit, as the Lord uses Brenda to minister to the heart of women."

Pastor Steve Smith, New Destiny Christian Church, Gadsden, AL

"Have you ever wondered what it would be like if Jesus were to speak freely to you of His deep love and affection? *Whispers from His Heart* speaks life and truth right to the heart, directly from the heart of our Lord and Savior. These *Whispers* are encouraging and empowering, delivering the message of God's relentless pursuit of YOU, His beloved child. Wherever you may be in your journey with Christ, it's time for the voice of God to bring you hope and healing. I cannot wait to dive into this devotional with the women in my Bible Reading Group."

Haley Hatchell, Women's Ministry Leader, Kairos Brentwood Baptist Church, Brentwood, TN

"Oh Brenda, I love your writing! It came to me at a time when I needed it so badly. I will utilize this as a group study with my Women's Ministry Team. It speaks to the heart of women no matter where they are in their lives. I especially liked the writing about letting go of the past. In my opinion, this is a winner!"

Brenda Chappell, Women's Ministry Director CrossPointe Church, Madison AL

"I don't know about you, but the longer I walk with the Lord, the more I understand the need of staying under the Wing of the Almighty! Seeking His presence and embrace is a necessity of life. Reading these *Whispers* that Brenda so graciously wrote helps me do that! They are not only encouraging and uplifting but also remind me of why it is so very important to "be still and know that He is God", Abba Father! Thank you, Brenda, for these nuggets from His heart. May all who read them be blessed."

Debbie Looper, Counseling Assistant, Urban, M*pact Pastor Rock Family Worship Center, Huntsville, Alabama

To:

_____

From:

_____

EXPERIENCING THE LOVE OF GOD

Whispers
from His Heart

Brenda W. Powell

Published by Morning Glory Enterprises. For information,
please email info@brendawpowell.com.

Cover and book design by Barbara A. Kilgore

Library of Congress Control Number: 2017915425

ISBN 978-0-9907514-6-5

Printed in the United States of America

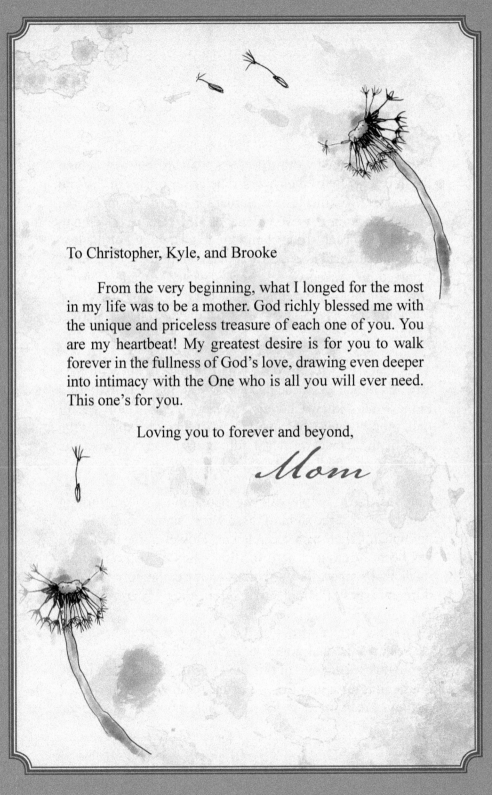

To Christopher, Kyle, and Brooke

From the very beginning, what I longed for the most in my life was to be a mother. God richly blessed me with the unique and priceless treasure of each one of you. You are my heartbeat! My greatest desire is for you to walk forever in the fullness of God's love, drawing even deeper into intimacy with the One who is all you will ever need. This one's for you.

Loving you to forever and beyond,

Mom

Preface

Within an author's writing projects lies a greater story behind the development of their work. The cover of *Whispers* is no exception. My illustrator, Barbara Kilgore, designed the original cover nearly two years ago. I loved it, was sold on it, and then . . . I felt God prompt me to change it. For the first time, Barbara and I both drew a blank at this new beginning. I prayed and asked God to reveal what He wanted on the cover. For months, we emailed back and forth possible ideas, but nothing seemed to fit. We waited on God and His perfect timing.

Then one day, I received an email from Barbara with new artwork. When I saw the dandelion with its seeds scattering in the wind, I knew God answered my prayer. But it wasn't until months later when my daughter, Brooke, explained the uses of the dandelion that I fully comprehended what the cover exemplified.

You see, most people call the dandelion a weed, turning their nose up at the sight of these wispy statues that show up uninvited in their lush green lawns. However, the dandelion has been a treasured herb for thousands of years. It offers medicinal support for our bodies and is commonly found in different types of herbal teas and remedies. I was amazed!

God is the healer of our soul. His love saves us, redeems us, restores us, and comforts us. It is the message woven throughout each page in this devotional. God's Word is the seed going forth into the soil of hearts in need of hope and healing, breathing new life into each day with His gentle whispers.

Table of Contents

From My Heart to Yours

My friend,

It is in the uncomfortable places where we experience true intimacy with God as we draw ever near to Him. In heightened times of despair, the Comforter comes and ministers His tender touch as only He can. As we give our all to the Master Healer with hearts desperate to receive His mercy, grace, and forgiveness, the broken pieces of our lives will begin to be transformed and put back together, ever so carefully. Bit by bit, moment by moment—we are a masterpiece in the making. The next time you are squeezed, pushed outside of your comfort zone, or stretched beyond what you think you can bear, recognize that what you are experiencing is an invitation to walk closer with the Father and discover the hidden gifts and beautiful manifestation of His glory in your life.

The *Whispers* from this devotional journal are excerpts from my personal walk written during my quiet times with the Lord as He spoke softly to my heart. They were written during difficult times—times of refinement, strengthening, and growth. Many were like a love song; other times I received discipline knowing I was circling that mountain once more while not wanting to, my bare heart exposed. But so many times the Word encouraged me and lifted me high. Looking back, I see that my journals are a gift that, if shared, can uplift, encourage, and inspire others on their own journey with God along their purposed path.

It is my heartfelt prayer that this devotional awakens your heart's desire to the beauty of time spent with Almighty God every day of your life. Get to know Jesus as never before and experience a relationship with Him that surpasses anything you have ever known.

 May these *Whispers* be like a warm blanket that holds you close, and may you soar on wings of God's everlasting and far-reaching love.

Brenda

Be still, and know that I am God . . .
Psalms 46:10

Let the gentle breeze flowing from the breath of God speak to you in the stillness. Listen to His voice. Know that He is your God.

Step Into a New Beginning

*T*his is a season of new beginnings, change, and power. It is a time when you will need to be clearly connected to My Spirit. He will lead you, so be careful to listen for His voice and obey.

Cast off reasoning. Shut down logic. Walk in faith with your gaze focused on Me and My Word. This is a period of great learning and preparation. This path is not easy; you must dig deep and rely on Me for your strength. I am your source for everything. Avoid the trap of trying to do things your way and in your time. Listen for My voice and follow My path. The rewards are great, so do not give up!

Believe, My daughter, only believe! Stay ever close to Me and I will give you the grace to overcome. You are more than a conqueror through My Son, Jesus, and you can do all things through Him! Quiet your soul, your mind, and your body. Rest in My strong arms as you bask in My glory, receiving the strength you need to press forward.

Now, arise refreshed and walk forth in the power of My Spirit. Let your mouth be full of praise, your heart bursting with song, and My joy flowing like a river. Abundance is yours when you follow Me.

I am here for you,

Your loving Father

"Forget the former things; do not dwell on the past. See, I am doing a new thing! Now it springs up; do you not perceive it? I am making a way in the desert and streams in the wasteland."
Isaiah 43:18-19

Serve wholeheartedly, as if you were serving the Lord, not men, because you know that the Lord will reward everyone for whatever good he does, whether he is slave or free.
Ephesians 6:7-8

No, in all these things we are more than conquerors through him who loved us.
Romans 8:37

Pause and Pray

Father, I thank you that You know my every need, and when I am unsure of which way to turn, You are always there, whispering into my heart which path I need to take. I praise You for Your faithfulness! I thank you for the Holy Spirit who fills me with power to do all that You call me to do and be. I give my all to You today to be used for Your glory.

From My Heart to Yours

As I take this first step, what am I believing God will do in my life? How can I prepare my heart to receive God's best?

_____

_____

_____

_____

_____

_____

_____

_____

_____

_____

_____

_____

_____

_____

_____

_____

_____

_____

Whispers

You Are
His Precious Treasure

*Y*ou are Mine, beloved. I have sealed you with the Holy Spirit for eternity. Though the mountains will be shaken and this earth will pass away, My love for you is unending. For I have made you in My image and likeness—a treasure that is precious! I see not what you are, but what you will become and what you are transforming into day by day as you renew your mind with My Word.

I look for you in the morning and, as you seek My face, I hold you close under the shelter of My wings. The song of praise in your heart spills from your lips; the pure joy that fills My throne room. I created you to worship Me and the sound of your surrender is ever so sweet.

My daughter, always and forever will I care for you, protect you, and walk with you through every fiery trial. And when tears fall down your face, I will gently wipe them away and caress your heart with hope, to heal and restore your soul.

You are loved, sweet child, with a love so deep and vast that you cannot comprehend its greatness or magnificence. I am here for you … eternally.

My arms are open,

Your loving Father

He who dwells in the shelter of the Most High will rest in the shadow of the Almighty. I will say of the Lord, "He is my refuge and my fortress, my God, in whom I trust."
Psalm 91:1-2

You have made known to me the paths of life; you will fill me with joy in your presence.
Acts 2:28

If I rise on the wings of the dawn, if I settle on the far side of the sea even there your hand will guide me, your right hand will hold me fast.
Psalm 139:9

Pause and Ponder

Spend time with the One who holds you in the palm of His hand. May God's Word be a gentle breeze that blows gently across your soul as He lavishes His love upon you today.

From My Heart to Yours

How can I still my heart and hear from the Father?
Do I fully recognize displays of His power in my daily walk?

_____

_____

_____

_____

_____

_____

_____

_____

_____

_____

_____

_____

_____

_____

_____

_____

_____

_____

_____

_____

Sail on
High Seas of Love

*W*hen you feel unsure and alone, precious one, be still and slowly inhale My enveloping love until your soul is saturated with the knowledge that I am always with you. Doing so throughout your day reminds you of My deep love along your journey in this frantic world of decisions and uncertainties.

If you feel like a tiny dot in the vast ocean of life, you are not alone. I am bigger than anything you face. There is no storm, no wave, and no tsunami of fear that can bury you beneath the fury of its attack.

Fully depend on Me, child, to carry you through. As you sit in your lifeboat, resist the temptation to pick up the oars and row toward the destination you desire. The harder you row away from Me and My will for your life, the more difficult your efforts will be as you strain against the current of obedience.

How long will you battle the waves? How many times will you climb back into the boat when it capsizes from failures, disappointment, and regret? My love anchors your soul and stills the raging seas tossing you to and fro. Lay down your oars. Lift your face to behold My glory. Wait for Me in your lifeboat to blow the sails propelling you toward the ultimate destination I have chosen.

Find strength in the warm rays of grace soaking into your soul. Glide through the calm waters of restoration and abundant life that come from a fully-surrendered heart. Sailing on the high seas of My love brings contentment, joy, and a life drenched in blessings.

Will you put down your oars and wait expectantly for Me to be the wind in your sails? My love never fails and endures beyond the existence of time.

I am the Wind in your sails,

Your loving Father

I will lead the blind by ways they have not known, along unfamiliar paths I will guide them; I will turn the darkness into light before them and make the rough places smooth. These are the things I will do; I will not forsake them.
Isaiah 42:16

As the eyes of slaves look to the hand of their master, as the eyes of a maid look to the hand of her mistress, so our eyes look to the Lord our God, till he shows us his mercy.
Psalm 123:2

Great peace have they who love your law, and nothing can make them stumble. I wait for your salvation, O Lord, and I follow your commands. I obey your statutes, for I love them greatly. I obey your precepts and your statutes, for all my ways are known to you.
Psalm 119: 165-168

Pause and Ponder

Why waste another moment living life your way when the oars of peace, freedom and fulfillment are calling you to grab hold and row? I encourage you to sail on, sister, in wild abandon on the high seas of God's love, rowing joyfully toward your destiny on the horizon that is ordained by God especially for you. Stay with the current of obedience and blessings will abound!

From My Heart to Yours

Lord, I have grown weary from trying to steer my own ship in life's turbulent waters. Today, I will lay down my oars and trust You to navigate my path in the following areas:

_____

_____

_____

_____

_____

_____

_____

_____

_____

_____

Dwell in His Presence

How precious is your time with Me, My child. It is a special sacrifice that pleases Me. Your praise and devotion to Me is a fragrant incense drifting into My presence. When you seek Me, you will find Me, and I will impart My wisdom to you. I will unlock hidden treasures and teach you many things during our time together.

In My presence, you will find life and all you need for the day. Rest in My love and mercy—they are new every day. Yield to Me completely and see the wonders I have for you.

Stay close to Me, child, and let Me work through you. You are My chosen vessel I will use to serve others. You will bring encouragement and life to those in need. Listen for My voice and speak the words I whisper to your heart. Let My love pour out of you to bless and strengthen those I place in the path of your garden.

Keep your mind and heart pure. Let humility help you walk holy and blameless, a beacon of light for the world to see and know that I am God.

How I treasure you,

Your loving Father

Enter his gates with thanksgiving and his courts with praise; give thanks to him and praise his name.
Psalm 100:4

Flee the evil desires of youth, and pursue righteousness, faith, love and peace, along with those who call on the Lord out of a pure heart.
2 Timothy 2:22

Remind the people to be subject to rulers and authorities, to be obedient, to be ready to do whatever is good, to slander no one, to be peaceable and considerate, and to show true humility toward all men.
Titus 3:1-2

Pause and Ponder

Treasures from the heart are like droplets of inspiration that water faith and bloom hope. Paint the canvas of your life with brushstrokes of compassion, vibrant colors of love, and textures of humility. You are a created masterpiece framed with perfection by the Master Artist.

From My Heart to Yours

What are some practical ways I can draw closer to my Heavenly Father?

_____

_____

_____

_____

_____

_____

_____

_____

_____

_____

_____

_____

_____

_____

_____

_____

_____

_____

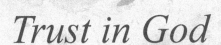

Trust in God

*T*rust. That one word has the power to set you free from worry and anxiety that keeps you up at night like vicious wolves snapping at your feet waiting to devour you.

Trust in Me, daughter. Trust Me with your tomorrows. Trust Me with the details of your day. When the troubles of this world threaten to pull you under, trusting in Me pulls you out of the quicksand of fear, doubt, and worry. My grace will wash away the gritty residue of your cares as I pull you out of the slimy pit of worry. You are My child and I never meant for you to live life this way.

Cast your cares on Me, beloved. Release your grip on the burdens never meant for you to carry. When you do, My peace floods your soul. Your mind is set free to focus on things that are lovely, pure, admirable, and noble. A freshness in your spirit takes hold empowering you to see with new eyes and hear with new ears.

Don't live your life shackled by fear any longer. Like a small child, trust Me with all of your heart. You cannot gain spiritual ground when you trust yourself to take care of life's worries. Give Me your concerns and walk hand in hand with Me through this day. I give each day as a special love gift to enjoy.

Will you trust Me? Will you draw near to Me—the One who loves you endlessly—and lay your burdens at My feet? My arms are ready to carry you through anything you face.

The ever-steadfast and faithful One,

Your loving Father

Those who know your name will trust in you, for
you, Lord, have never forsaken
those who seek you.
Psalm 9:10

Surely God is my salvation; I will trust and not
be afraid. The Lord, the Lord, is my strength and
my song; he has become my salvation.
Isaiah 12:2

Trust in him at all times, O people; pour out your
hearts to him, for God is our refuge.
Psalm 62:8

Pause and Ponder

Trust God to hold **all** the moments of your life. Glance back over your shoulder to everything He has brought you through and all the blessings He has so graciously rained down on you. Remember, and give thanks. Then trust and believe!

From My Heart to Yours

What is the rear-view mirror of your past revealing to you today?

_____

_____

_____

_____

_____

_____

_____

_____

_____

_____

_____

_____

_____

_____

_____

_____

_____

_____

His Perfect Peace

When you are in the eye of life's hurricane, do not take your eyes off of Me. Without My peace, daughter, the chaos in your soul escalates until you are spinning out of control. You cannot make right decisions when in this state of confusion. I am not the author of confusion! When you find yourself outside the realm of My perfect peace, realize that you are standing on Satan's fertile soil of destruction.

Pay attention to what is happening around you. Stop and reflect on what is causing the turmoil in your life. Satan's strategies are targeted at you, your family, and your finances with pin-point precision. Open wide your spiritual eyes and discern where your battle lies. Recognize the warning signs and be quick to discipline yourself to return to the safe haven of My peace and rest under the shelter of My mighty wings.

Be watchful for the gradual pulling away from My protective care and do not wait until you're spinning mindlessly out of control before calling out My name. Keep watch over the door of your lips and heart. My perfect peace will keep you calm in the midst of your storm.

The Peace in your storm,

Your loving Father

The fruit of righteousness will be peace; the effect of righteousness will be quietness and confidence forever.
Isaiah 32:17

Find rest, O my soul, in God alone; my hope comes from him. He alone is my rock and my salvation; he is my fortress,
I will not be shaken.
Psalm 62:5-6

Set a guard over my mouth, O Lord; keep watch over the door of my lips. Let not my heart be drawn to what is evil, to take part in wicked deeds with men who are evildoers; let me not eat of their delicacies.
Psalm 141:3-4

Pause and Ponder

Replenish the soil of your heart daily with God's vibrant and fertile Word that will make the disease of Satan's lies and deception harder to penetrate. When circumstances seem daunting, seek rest under the protection of His mighty wings. Crawl into the open arms of Jesus and let His grace, His peace, wash over you and renew your mind from worry and the constant onslaught of lies beating you down.

From My Heart to Yours

Lord, I am ready to rest in Your perfect peace. Today, I will make peace a priority in these areas of my life:

_____

_____

_____

_____

_____

_____

_____

_____

_____

_____

_____

_____

_____

_____

_____

_____

_____

_____

_____

You Are

*Y*our heart is searching, daughter, for truth . . . My truth. Here, in the stillness of the morning, you will find Me as you seek Me with all of your heart.

I see your hungry heart full of questions longing for the truth of My Word. Humbly you came with no more pretenses, impure motives, or selfish ambition as you sit faithfully at My feet to receive My Word that feeds your famished soul with lasting food.

When you come before Me with a heart laid bare and broken, this is when I can do My most beautiful work. Gently I will speak to your heart, lovingly I will reshape you, and you will stand firmly on the Rock of your salvation.

My breath of hope blows softly across your troubled soul, building upon each intake until you rise again in the power of who you are in Me. The truth of My Word declares that you are more than a conqueror through Christ Jesus, you are My dearly loved child that shines like a bright star in the universe, and you are victorious in The One who died for your sins.

My Word stands forever and does not change. Oh, the pearls of wisdom waiting to be discovered as you dive into the depths of My living Word! Peel back layer after layer, going deeper still, until you uncover the answers you have been seeking.

All you need is before you as we meet in our special place of fellowship. My heart beating against yours, My love holding you close, and My streams of mercy washing over you as grace ministers to your aching soul.

You are My cherished child. All I have is yours and you belong to Me. I love you completely, passionately, and eternally.

The Healer of your heart,

Your loving Father

How priceless is your unfailing love! Both high and low among men find refuge in the shadow of your wings. They feast on the abundance of your house; you give them drink from your river of delights. For with you is the fountain of life; in your light we see light.
Psalm 36:7-9

As for God, his way is perfect; the word of the Lord is flawless. He is a shield for all who take refuge in him. For who is God besides the Lord? And who is the Rock except our God?
2 Samuel 22:31-32

I pray that out of his glorious riches he may strengthen you with power through his Spirit in your inner being, so that Christ may dwell in your hearts through faith . . . .
Ephesians 3:16-17

Pause and Pray

Father, how I praise You for Your endless love that runs so deep for me. My heart is full of thanks that I can come to You just as I am—weary, broken and in need of Your gentle touch. I will praise You all of my days for the gift of Jesus— my salvation—and Your mercy that is new every single day. All I need is You, Father. You are more than enough!

From My Heart to Yours

How will I rest today knowing who I am and Whose I am?

_____

_____

_____

_____

_____

_____

_____

_____

_____

_____

_____

_____

Cultivate Your Garden

*L*iving a life of love requires shifting focus from yourself to others. Open your spiritual eyes today and see what I see. Your life takes on a whole new meaning when selfishness turns into selflessness.

When you stand with arms wide open in constant readiness to meet people's needs, it reflects a life devoted to Me, and eternal rewards will be yours. Do not be overwhelmed with the vast needs that extend all over the world. Faithfully minister in your sphere of influence. Carefully cultivate the garden of souls around you waiting to be harvested, ripe and ready to receive My love.

Awaken to each day with a heart overflowing with thankfulness. Be full of joy knowing you have been graced with one more day of precious, abundant life. Make every moment count for My glory.

Beloved, choose to live in peace and unity. This world is waiting for a touch from Me that will flow through you, My chosen vessel.

Sow seeds joyfully today,

Your loving Father

Do nothing out of selfish ambition or vain conceit, but in humility consider others better than yourselves. Each of you should look not only to your own interests, but also to the interests of others.
Philippians 2:3-4

"You did not choose me, but I chose you and appointed you to go and bear fruit—fruit that will last. Then the Father will give you whatever you ask in my name. This is my command: Love each other."
John 15:16-17

Be imitators of God, therefore, as dearly loved children and live a life of love, just as Christ loved us and gave himself up for us as a fragrant offering and sacrifice to God.
Ephesians 5:1-2

Pause and Ponder

When the aroma of God's love permeates the air around us—following us wherever we go—people will be drawn to the irresistible scent of Heaven and will want to partake of its sweetness and taste the eternal life of Jesus baked to perfection inside of us.

From My Heart to Yours

How can I make myself available to others today? What opportunities are around me where I can be of service or help someone in need?

_____

_____

_____

_____

_____

_____

_____

_____

_____

_____

_____

_____

_____

_____

_____

_____

_____

_____

Whispers

The Master Conductor

Oh, My child, I see you running to and fro, frantic in your efforts to help Me make things happen. How many times will you go around that mountain of unbelief? Yes, unbelief! That may surprise you, but it's true. You have a part to play in the symphony of life, but when you try to play all of the instruments rather than your own, well, the sound is loudly off-tune and unpleasant.

I am the Master Conductor, and I strategically place people and events in their reserved seats in the orchestra of your life. Your zeal and passion are commendable, but when they consume you, your sound becomes off-key and affects the composition of your life's soundtrack.

I am your *First* Love. I should be your waking thought when you rise and the final applause as you drift off to sleep. I will not be replaced by anything in your life. Hear Me, child. Repent and get back into your seat so I can play you loud and strong. Your repentant heart and obedience is what I desire above all.

Come, let Me fine tune you once more so you can continue to run your race in perfect harmony with the hand-picked orchestra I have selected for you. May you overflow with hope so you can soar to higher heights as My grace falls like rain and soaks your spirit with faith.

The show must go on,

Your loving Father

"*Yet I hold this against you: You have forsaken your first love. Remember the height from which you have fallen! Repent and do the things you did at first. If you do not repent, I will come to you and remove your lampstand from its place.*"
Revelation 2:4-5

But Samuel replied: "Does the Lord delight in burnt offerings and sacrifices as much as in obeying the voice of the Lord? To obey is better than sacrifice, and to heed is better than the fat of rams."
1 Samuel 15:22

We wait in hope for the Lord; he is our help and our shield. In him our hearts rejoice, for we trust in his holy name. May your unfailing love rest upon us, O Lord, even as we put our hope in you.
Psalm 33:20-22

Pause and Ponder

God is your music and He writes the soundtracks of your life. Let go and let God, for when you live in obedience, you position yourself for blessings. A simple shift of focus can turn an otherwise gloomy day into one full of radiant hope and promise.

From My Heart to Yours

Lord, I want You to write the beautiful soundtrack to my life. Today, I will quiet my soul and listen for the first note of Your musical masterpiece.

_____

_____

_____

_____

_____

_____

_____

_____

_____

_____

_____

_____

_____

_____

_____

_____

_____

_____

_____

_____

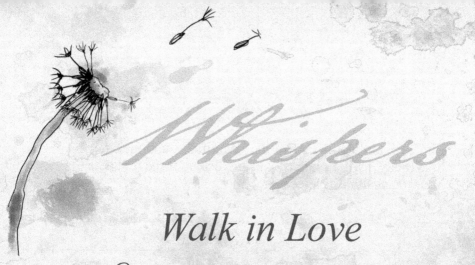

Walk in Love

Serve with gladness, My child, for this pleases Me. As you go through your day, look for ways to serve others. When you are helping and serving others, it is as if you are serving Me. Do this without grumbling or complaining. Renew your mind with this truth. Find joy in even the simplest of things knowing that this pleases and honors Me.

As you open your heart to serve others, you are sowing seeds along the way for eternity. How I love to pour out My Spirit, water those seeds, and watch them grow! At the proper time, those seeds will produce a harvest if you do not allow yourself to get weary and give up. Rejoice, for you are My chosen vessel! Take no thought for yourself or what is or is not fair. Just obey My voice when I whisper into your soul and remember that everything you do or say is for My glory.

Your harvest is coming with abundant seed to sow. Take joy in what I have chosen for you and use your gifts to bring glory and honor to Me and My Kingdom.

The Master Farmer,

Your loving Father

*Serve wholeheartedly, as if you were serving the
Lord, not men, because you know that the Lord
will reward everyone for whatever good he does,
whether he is slave or free.*
Ephesians 6:7-8

*Let us not become weary in doing good,
for at the proper time we will reap a harvest
if we do not give up.*
Galatians 6:9

*Do nothing out of selfish ambition or vain
conceit, but in humility consider others better
than yourselves. Each of you should look not
only to your own interests, but also to the
interest of others. Your attitude should be the
same as that of Christ Jesus.*
Philippians 2:3-5

*Each one should use whatever gift he has
received to serve others, faithfully administering
God's grace in its various forms.*
1 Peter 4:10

Pause and Ponder

Purpose to walk in God's love each and every day; live
sacrificially to better the life of another person. What
exactly does that look like? It is compassion with shoes on
to actively help those in need.

From My Heart to Yours

How can I serve others today? What opportunities are ripe for sowing seed into someone's life?

_____

_____

_____

_____

_____

_____

_____

_____

_____

_____

_____

_____

_____

_____

_____

_____

_____

_____

Experiencing Joy Untold

*D*aughter, each day of life is a rare gift, as is every tiny detail that happens along the way—the spectacular sunrise, the unexpected warm smile from a grocery clerk, the tinkling sound of a child's laughter. All of these things will cause joy to bubble up in your heart if you will but recognize them for what they are—love gifts from your Abba Father. Let your heart be forever thankful and rejoice in each detail that occurs throughout your day's journey, no matter how small and insignificant it may seem.

Learning to live this way as a lifestyle, My child, will result in everlasting happiness that spreads joy to all those around you, bringing glory to My name. You will experience a fullness of a love that is so great, so far-reaching, that **you know that you know** nothing will ever separate you from Me.

I am always near and I care about every part of your life. I have numbered the hairs on your head and I know you . . . from top to toe and beginning to end. I created you to enjoy your life to the fullest, as I abide in you and you abide in Me. Walk with Me in anticipation of a day that is brimming over with My blessings.

When trials come along (and they will), rejoice and know that I am refining your character and empowering you to soar higher and higher with Me.

Holding you close,

Your loving Father

Be joyful always; pray continually; give thanks in all circumstances, for this is God's will for you in Christ Jesus.
1 Thessalonians 5:16

Your love, O Lord, reaches to the heavens, your faithfulness to the skies.
Psalm 36:5

For you have been my hope, O Sovereign Lord, my confidence since my youth. From birth I have relied on you; you brought me forth from my mother's womb. I will ever praise you.
Psalm 71:5-6

Pause and Ponder

Always remember and purpose to dance through life, keeping your eyes on Him, and your heart overflowing with love and thankfulness. Then you won't be able to stop that extra bounce in your step . . . and, you just might find yourself twirling.

From My Heart to Yours

How will I stir up the joy in my heart and let it set the tone for my day/life?

_____

_____

_____

_____

_____

_____

_____

_____

_____

_____

_____

_____

_____

_____

_____

_____

_____

_____

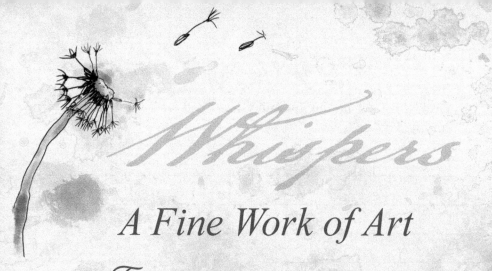

Whispers

A Fine Work of Art

*E*xamine yourself. Examine your motives. Dig deeply into the **why** behind everything you do and the condition of your heart will be revealed.

When pursuing the dreams of your heart, even the best of intentions can become twisted into something that is not meant to be.

Not trusting in Me becomes striving within your own strength. The mission, the ministry, and the dream becomes the focus instead of ME. Reposition yourself and line up with My will for your life. Release the preconceived picture you have of your life. Let Me, the Master Artist, paint the beautiful illustration of what your life—planned before you were ever created—is supposed to be. I paint the brush strokes of each day, a masterpiece in the making, until the time when I add the final touch … that last color finishing the work I've called you to do: a legacy resulting in **My** glory magnified, **My** love lighting the darkness, **My** salvation reaching multitudes. **Your** life well-lived. **Your** race ran victoriously.

Embrace each day with My joy untold. Fill your heart with the promises of My Word and let faith lead each step you take knowing it is the great I AM that colors your life with detailed strokes of perfection.

The Master Artist,

Your loving Father

*All a man's ways seem innocent to him, but
motives are weighed by the LORD.*
Proverbs 16:2

*Trust in the LORD with all your heart and lean
not on your own understanding; in all your ways
acknowledge him, and he will make
your paths straight.*
Proverbs 3: 5-6

*Yet he did not waver through unbelief regarding
the promise of God, but was strengthened in
his faith and gave glory to God, being fully
persuaded that God had power to do
what he had promised.*
Romans 4:20-21

Pause and Pray

Father, please forgive me when I strive in my own might and
try to make things happen on my own. You are my All in All
and the One that colors my world with perfection. May Your
will be done in my life, today and always.

From My Heart to Yours

Father, today I will join You in creating a beautiful masterpiece. What can I do today to manifest God's colorful experiences in my life?

_____

_____

_____

_____

_____

_____

_____

_____

_____

_____

_____

_____

_____

_____

_____

_____

_____

Whispers

Arise
Courageous and Bold

When fear comes knocking at your door, do not shrink back in defeat and allow yourself to be overcome by the enemy. At its first insistent knock, speak My Word and declare My victory that has already been won. Use this mighty weapon to defeat the enemy before he can pierce you with one of his fiery darts.

Meditate on My Word, which is the Sword of the Spirit, and allow it to soak into the deep recesses of your being so that when the enemy attacks, you will be ready and armed for battle. Fear not, precious one, for when you draw near to Me, I will draw near to you. Call out the name of Jesus—the Name that is above all names—full of power and might. He is your source for everything you need. Stand your ground and declare that I have not given you a spirit of fear but of power, love, and a sound mind. Then watch the Deceiver crawl back into his pit! Remind the one who rises to torment you that he is a defeated foe under your feet through the mighty blood of Jesus that covers you as My dearly loved child.

Victory is won, daughter, so stand firm in your faith and rebuke the lies of the enemy. Turn your eyes to Jesus, your Redeemer, and praise Him for all He has done for you. Thank Him for His love, His power, and His strength that became yours through His sacrificial death at the cross. Defeat the enemy with overflowing praise from your lips and a heart full of thanks.

Awaken and rise up as a lioness—bold and beautiful because of who you are in Me. Roar out the power of My Word and send the enemy fleeing in all directions. For what started as fear will turn into rejoicing.

Always standing by your side,

Your loving Father

Submit yourselves, then, to God. Resist the devil, and he will flee from you. Come near to God and he will come near to you.
James 4:7-8

Therefore God exalted him to the highest place and gave him the name that is above every name, that at the name of Jesus every knee should bow, in heaven and on earth and under the earth, and every tongue confess that Jesus Christ is Lord, to the glory of God the Father.
Philippians 2:9-11

So do not fear, for I am with you; do not be dismayed, for I am your God. I will strengthen you and help you; I will uphold you with my righteous right hand.
Isaiah 41:10

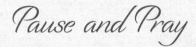

Pause and Pray

Father, You are the anchor of my soul, the very breath that keeps me alive. Though fear and obstacles screaming defeat stand tall, it is You, O God, that helps me overcome them all. As You fill my sometimes fearful heart with songs of praise, I will raise hands to You in thankfulness, for You are faithful! I choose to praise my way to victory today.

From My Heart to Yours

Today, I choose to stand confident and victorious. What steps will I take today to make bold, courageous steps forward in my faith and life?

_____

_____

_____

_____

_____

_____

_____

_____

_____

_____

_____

_____

_____

_____

A Blessed
Life of Obedience

*Y*our obedience, My child, is more pleasing to Me than any sacrifice you make. When you are quick to obey, it perfumes the air with a sweet aroma that fills My sanctuary. As you draw closer to Me and understand Me intimately, obeying My voice will come as natural to you as every breath you take. When we are truly connected, you will radiate with My glory and all that you do will be done at your best—as unto Me. Fill your mind with good things. Meditate on My Word, sing songs of praise to Me, lift holy hands to heaven, and worship Me with all that is in you—every day and throughout your day.

When I am first in your life, you will experience life at its fullest. My joy will sweep across your soul and sing a heavenly chorus so pure and so beautiful that Christ's righteousness cannot help but pour out of you in rivers of living water. Humble yourself before Me this day and live the blessed life of obedience.

The Author and Finisher of your faith,

Your loving Father

But Samuel replied: "Does the LORD delight in burnt offerings and sacrifices as much as in obeying the voice of the LORD? To obey is better than sacrifice, and to heed is better than the fat of rams."
1 Samuel 15:22

Finally, brothers and sisters, whatever is true, whatever is noble, whatever is right, whatever is pure, whatever is lovely, whatever is admirable— if anything is excellent or praiseworthy—think about such things.
Philippians 4:8

"But seek first his kingdom and his righteousness, and all these things will be given to you as well."
Matthew 6:33

Pause and Ponder

When you live in obedience, you position yourself for blessings. As God becomes your delight, He will lovingly give you the desires of your heart. May you choose to look through the rosy lens of heaven throughout your day instead of the tainted glasses of your own agenda and expectations. As you do, life will look a whole lot brighter!

From My Heart to Yours

What challenges or obstacles do I need to lay at the Father's feet? How can my obedience be the touchstone for His handiwork in my life?

_____

_____

_____

_____

_____

_____

_____

_____

_____

_____

_____

_____

_____

_____

_____

_____

_____

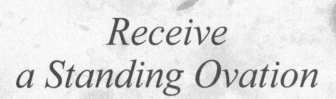

Receive
a Standing Ovation

*D*aughter, what if you had only one day left in your life? What would you focus on? What would you do?

Reflect on these questions. Your answers will reveal the condition of your heart, giving you better perspective for the changes you need to make on your life journey. Embrace this way of thinking, for I have not promised you an endless supply of tomorrows.

Do not waste precious time chasing after the demands of this world. Turn a deaf ear to her seductive words; they only serve to pull you into a deceptive trap that will suffocate you with lies. Rather, listen with your spiritual ears for My voice that will lead you into all Truth.

My path of love calls out to you to run with vigor and perseverance each minute of every day, being vigilant to make loving stops along the way to care for and help those who are in need.

If you had but one day left in which to leave your imprint on this world, let it be full of embracing others with My love, abiding in My presence, and being in constant worship of Me.

Meditate on this, My child, and allow My Spirit to lead you into the full life I created for you. Live for Me and My glory each day, and when your journey has reached its final destination, your life lived through My love will receive a standing ovation.

Press in and press on,

Your loving Father

And he has given us this command: Whoever loves God must also love his brother.
1 John 4:21

The world and its desires pass away, but the man who does the will of God lives forever.
1 John 2:17

Therefore, since we are surrounded by such a great cloud of witnesses, let us throw off everything that hinders and the sin that so easily entangles, and let us run with perseverance the race marked for us.
Hebrews 12:1

Pause and Ponder

Paint rainbows into people's lives and watch them light up and sparkle. Make your world a better place by becoming the love of God as you serve Him and others and multiply joy.

From My Heart to Yours

What can I do today that will leave a legacy, an impression on those God wants me to bless?

_____

_____

_____

_____

_____

_____

_____

_____

_____

_____

_____

_____

_____

_____

_____

_____

_____

_____

_____

_____

Find Strength in Him

*B*reathe in the heavenly aroma of My presence, child, as you sit quietly and listen for the whisper of My voice to your heart. Holy communion with Me sustains and strengthens you in times of trouble and fills your heart with joy.

May your heart always be hungry for Me and your soul thirsty for My Word—the Living Water that never runs dry.

Draw near to Me and lean into My arms that long to hold you close and secure. I will comfort you and flood your soul with My peace when you cast your cares and anxieties into My strong, capable hands. There is no decision, thought, or worry too large or small for Me. I care about **everything** in your life and I desire to be Lord over **all** of you.

When you relinquish control of the seemingly insignificant details of everyday life, as well as the mountains that loom large in your path, then you will find the sweet peace Jesus promised. My overflowing joy will give you strength to live each day to the fullest.

Sit awhile in the beauty of My presence as My peace and joy refill your empty soul so you can rise anew.

My precious child, how I love you. You are MINE!

Sustaining you always,

Your loving Father

You have made known to me the path of life; you will fill me with joy in your presence, with eternal pleasures at your right hand.
Psalm 16:11

"Therefore I tell you, do not worry about your life, what you will eat or drink; or about your body, what you will wear. Is not life more important than food, and the body more important than clothes? Look at the birds of the air; they do not sow or reap or store away in barns, and yet your heavenly Father feeds them. Are you not much more valuable than they? Who of you by worrying can add a single hour to his life?"
Matthew 6:25-27

"I have told you these things, so that in me you may have peace. In this world you will have trouble. But take heart! I have overcome the world."
John 16:33

Pause and Pray

Father, as I enter into Your presence, I come hungry for more of You. Please help me to sit still before You so I can hear Your whisper of love that will breathe life back into this world-weary heart of mine. Only You, O God, can quench the thirst within me as You fill my cup to overflowing with Your living waters of hope and perfect peace.

From My Heart to Yours

What do I need strength for today? What do I need to relinquish in order to experience God's peace?

_____

_____

_____

_____

_____

_____

_____

_____

_____

_____

_____

_____

_____

_____

_____

_____

_____

_____

Whispers

Forgiven and Free

*F*orgiveness. Such power in that one word. I sacrificed My only Son to bear all the sins of this world that were not His. He was blameless and pure, yet He willingly, and with a deep love for mankind, **chose** to suffer and die for you and all mankind so that you may have life. A gift freely given from a heart full of unconditional love that never ends.

When you became My child, you accepted this merciful gift. But I ask, do you forgive as I forgave you? Do you truly forgive those who have hurt or offended you? Do you cast their sins as far as the east is from the west to be remembered no more? Or do you replay the wrongs done against you like a broken record, repeating the offense over and over in the recesses of your mind as a tally sheet that grows longer whenever you are in the presence of the offender?

Check the pulse of your heart. Ask the Holy Spirit to reveal any unforgiveness that is strangling your heart and spreading poison into your soul. Resentment and bitterness are Satan's tools that destroy you from the inside out, twin destructive forces that will snuff out My light longing to shine brightly within you.

Sometimes the one you need to forgive is yourself. Jesus drank your cup of suffering with such great love in order for you to experience an abundant and free life in Him. Freely I gave, and freely you received. How can you do any less?

Let go of all past hurts. I am the Lover of your soul and in Me all things are made new. Walk in My love. Walk in total forgiveness and freedom. **Choose** life. **Choose** to live in overflowing joy and abundant living.

Overcome with Me,

Your loving Father

"For if you forgive men when they sin against you, your heavenly Father will also forgive you. But if you do not forgive men their sins, your Father will not forgive your sins."
Matthew 6:14-15

Get rid of all bitterness, rage and anger, brawling and slander, along with every form of malice. Be kind and compassionate to one another, forgiving each other, just as in Christ God forgave you.
Ephesians 4:31-32

"Forget the former things; do not dwell on the past. See, I am doing a new thing! Now it springs up; do you not perceive it? I am making a way in the desert and streams in the wasteland."
Isaiah 43:18-19

Pause and Ponder

The poison of bitterness robs a person of a joyful heart and instead makes it like an open, festering wound that is continuously painful. May you choose forgiveness and live life full of God's unimaginable joy—just like Jesus.

From My Heart to Yours

Lord, please forgive me for holding on to bitterness and anger. Help me see others as You do. Who do I need to forgive? How will that affect my life and theirs?

_____

_____

_____

_____

_____

_____

_____

_____

_____

_____

_____

_____

Radiate with Love

What is your life magnifying? My child, reflect deeply on this question and search your heart for truth. The heartbeat of heaven pulsates with My love, a radiant light that sets fire to your soul. A life-giving flame that never dies but is constantly fanned by your thankfulness and mindfulness as you walk forth in My love daily. A flame growing in stature until it can no longer be contained within the walls of your fragile body. My all-consuming love radiates through you and spills over onto the mission field of lost, hungry souls that exist in the world.

What may seem microscopic, incredibly small, and not even noteworthy to you might be the fresh breath of hope that sparks renewed life into a soul drowning in a sea of life-long disappointments. Never discount the value of one single act or word of kindness and love as you go along your way. Do not hesitate when I speak to your heart encouraging you to reach out to others whether you know them or not.

Again I ask, what is your life magnifying? Someone's eternal being might be saved.

Shine with My light,

Your loving Father

66

For this reason I remind you to fan into flame the gift of God, which is in you through the laying on of my hands. For God did not give us a spirit of timidity, but a spirit of power, of love and of self-discipline.
2 Timothy 1:6-7

Dear friends, since God so loved us, we also ought to love one another. No one has ever seen God; but if we love one another, God lives in us and his love is made complete in us.
1 John 4:11-12

Dear children, let us not love with words or tongue but with actions and in truth.
1 John 3:18

Pause and Ponder

Radiate today with the brilliant light of God's love. Be the flame that draws the lost to our Jesus' saving grace. May you be a stunning reflection of the awesome God that we serve!

From My Heart to Yours

Father, I want to magnify Your love in my life and the lives of others. How can I radiate Your love today?

_____

_____

_____

_____

_____

_____

_____

_____

_____

_____

_____

_____

_____

_____

_____

_____

_____

_____

_____

_____

_____

The Shepherd's Voice

*C*hosen one, My sheep hear My voice and follow the one they recognize. There are many voices clamoring for your attention throughout the day. Tune out distractions that vie to drown out My voice calling your name.

When you spend time with Me, you will come to know Me intimately and discern My voice above the others hammering in your ear and leading you astray. I AM the great Shepherd and My sheep follow Me with complete trust, loyalty, and a deep desire to please Me.

What voices are you listening to? The world's voice laced with lies telling you to seek your pleasure, your plan, and your way? Where are you seeking so-called wise counsel? Ask yourself these questions and diligently search your heart.

Spend time with Me. Run to the pages of My Word when problems arise and all of the answers you seek will be found. I know every petition before it leaves your lips, and there is no request or need that is too small or insignificant. I care about every part of you!

Come before Me. Share your heart with Me. Seek Me for answers when you are on your knees and you will hear My voice, the only Voice you should listen to. I am here to guide your every step.

When you can discern My voice over the constant buzz, there is peace knowing your Shepherd is watching, ready to steer you back into the flock should you go astray. My sheep hear My voice. Set your mind and heart to spend time in My presence every day. Then, and only then, will My voice ring clear above the hustle and bustle of this world.

The Ever-Watchful Shepherd,

Your loving Father

"My sheep listen to my voice; I know them, and they follow me. I give them eternal life, and they shall never perish; no one can snatch them out of my hand. My Father, who has given them to me, is greater than all; no one can snatch them out of my Father's hand. I and the Father are one."
John 10:27-30

I will sing to the Lord all my life; I will sing praise to my God as long as I live. May my meditation be pleasing to him, as I rejoice in the Lord.
Psalm 104:33-34

Whether you turn to the right or to the left, your ears will hear a voice behind you saying, "This is the way; walk in it."
Isaiah 30:21

Pause and Pray

I thank you, Father, that I am a little lamb You adore, protect, and guide. Help me draw ever closer to You so I'll always recognize Your gentle voice—my One, true Shepherd. I desire You above anything this world has to offer.

From My Heart to Yours

Lord, I choose to focus on spending time with You and listening for Your voice. Your words are guiding me to do the following today:

_____

_____

_____

_____

_____

_____

_____

_____

_____

_____

_____

_____

_____

A Heart Song of Praise

*M*y beloved, the depth of your praise pleases Me. A heart full of worship and thankfulness is what I desire. I inhabit the praise of My people and it is there where you will find Me. A passionate heart seeking to find Me, longing to taste of My goodness, will be ushered into My presence.

Come and dwell in My sanctuary. Let your mind unfurl from your frenzied pace as you rest in Me. No time constraints, just sweet communion with your Abba Father. My love whispers gently across the plains of your heart, bringing much-needed relief from the scorching winds of this hurried life.

Sing your love songs to Me, for they fill My throne room with beauty and light untold. Let go and worship Me with all that is in you. My grace will fall like rain over you when you open your heart and praise Me.

All that I have is yours,

Your loving Father

Taste and see that the Lord is good; blessed is the man who takes refuge in him. Fear the Lord, you his saints, for those who fear him lack nothing.
Psalm 34:8-9

The Lord is my strength and my shield; my heart trusts in him, and I am helped. My heart leaps for joy and I will give thanks to him in song.
Psalm 28:7

"Come to me, all you who are weary and burdened, and I will give you rest. Take my yoke upon you and learn from me, for I am gentle and humble in heart, and you will find rest for your souls. For My yoke is easy and my burden is light."
Matthew 11:28-30

Pause and Ponder

God's love is an anchor for our soul, and prayer connects us to our Heavenly Father who releases His power to meet our every need when we are on our knees.

From My Heart to Yours

What are the lyrics to my heart song for the Father? What words do I want my heart to sing to Him?

_____

_____

_____

_____

_____

_____

_____

_____

_____

_____

_____

_____

_____

_____

_____

_____

_____

Search Your Heart

*D*aughter, where are you spending your time? What thoughts consume your mind and fuel the feelings driving you throughout the day? Search your heart and let My spirit reveal the things you are putting in place of Me and our relationship. Lay down everything that is keeping you from My presence.

I am God Almighty and there will be no other gods before Me. I will not accept second place! Quiet your mind and sit still in My presence, child; listen for My voice. Attune your ears and listen closely to what I have to say. Put your hand in Mine with complete trust and watch what I will do.

Release your hold on anything in your life that is usurping My place. I am your Father and I long to give you good things, but obedience to My will and commandments is required. You must first lose your life before you will find it. In Me, life is abundant, full of joy, wrapped in peace, and overflowing with My love.

Fall into My open arms and experience abundant life. Do not hesitate. Let go and trust Me to catch you—I will not fail nor forsake you.

A firm Foundation and steady Hand,

Your loving Father

*K*now that the Lord has set apart the godly for
himself; the Lord will hear when I call to him.
In your anger do not sin; when you are on your
beds, search your hearts and be silent. Offer
right sacrifices and trust in the Lord.
Psalm 4:3-5

*T*his day I call heaven and earth as witnesses
against you that I have set before you life and
death, blessings and curses. Now choose life, so
that you and your children may live and that you
may love the Lord your God, listen to his voice,
and hold fast to him. For the Lord is your life,
and he will give you many years in the
land he swore to give to your fathers,
Abraham, Isaac and Jacob.
Deuteronomy 30: 19-20

*Y*ou have made known to me the path of life;
you will fill me with joy in your presence, with
eternal pleasures at your right hand.
Psalm 16:11

76

Pause and Pray

Father, shelter my heart today from those things in the world that would lead me astray. Empower me to shut out the ongoing racket in my head by sitting still before You. Attune my ears so I can hear the soft familiar voice of You, my Shepherd, calling me into Your place of rest. Help me keep my eyes on You and follow the path You have laid out for me this day.

From My Heart to Yours

Father, today I will focus my time by removing these hindrances from my life:

_____

_____

_____

_____

_____

_____

_____

_____

_____

_____

_____

_____

Whispers

Run to the Roar of Fear

What are you afraid of? What is it that frightens you, causing you to persistently hide? When fear is stuffed and buried beneath piles of pretense and wishful thinking, it doesn't disappear as you would hope. Instead, your fear smolders, flares up, and carries a constant stench of something burning deep on the inside.

When you accept Jesus as your Savior, you become an overcomer through the shed blood of Christ. His strength and resurrection power of the Holy Spirit is within you. Fear is a weapon of the enemy used to paralyze your soul from becoming all I created you to be.

Look to Me for your strength. Find in Me the courage you need to face your fears and overcome them. Declare every promise in My Word that is yours as My child and run to the roar of the fears that are binding you.

It is time to break free of the chains holding you back. Victory has already been won. Cast off the lies that have pinned you down, smothering the potential just waiting to be released from within. I have not given you a spirit of fear, but of power, love, and a sound mind. Rise tall and put on your armor and fight.

Do not throw away your confidence! I am with you and you will be victorious. As David ran toward Goliath, run to the roar and slay the fear giants tormenting you once and for all. Freedom is one faith step away. Will you load your sling and take that first step now?

Overcome with Me,

Your loving Father

You, dear children, are from God and have overcome them, because the one who is in you is greater than the one who is in the world.
1 John 4:4

So do not throw away your confidence; it will be richly rewarded. You need to persevere so that when you have done the will of God, you will receive what he has promised.
Hebrews 10:36

For God did not give us a spirit of timidity, but a spirit of power, of love and of self-discipline.
2 Timothy 1:7

Pause and Ponder

What lies from the enemy are stifling your life? Don't allow the poison of fear, doubt, and insecurity to fester in your mind, looming larger and larger until you're consumed with discouragement and hope disappears in a puff! Facing fear is the first step of faith that overcomes through the power of His grace. When mountains of fear or trials tower before you, remember all that God has done for you and, with His help, you can climb that steep mountain surefooted, determined, and with a song in your heart.

From My Heart to Yours

My Father, I will not be moved by fear because it has no hold on me. I am strong because You have proven Yourself faithful to me in the past. I am choosing to remember Your strong Hand in these moments:

_____

_____

_____

_____

_____

_____

_____

_____

_____

_____

_____

_____

_____

_____

_____

_____

_____

_____

_____

Balanced Perspective

$\mathcal{M}$y beloved, carefully examine your perspective and make sure it is not off-kilter. Don't be hasty and give up on the half-finished story of your life. Be ever watchful for Satan's carefully laid ambush at every corner, every fork in the road, and every road stop. The Deceiver hisses his lies that say you are unloved, forgotten, unworthy, lost, and defeated. His purpose is to steal, kill, and destroy you. Turn a deaf ear to his lies! My child, listen to My truth etched deeply in your heart that declares you are LOVED, PRECIOUS, WORTHY, FORGIVEN, REDEEMED, and VICTORIOUS!

You are more than a conqueror through Jesus. In Him, you have strength to overcome all attacks of the enemy on your soul.

Be ever mindful of the gratitude—or lack thereof—flowing from your heart and out the door of your lips. Being aware of what is spilling from your heart is a sure-fire indicator of who you are listening to: the hater of mankind, or Me, the Lover of your soul, your One, true God.

You belong to Me,

Your loving Father

81

For he has rescued us from the dominion of darkness and brought us into the kingdom of the Son he loves, in whom we have redemption, the forgiveness of sins.
Colossians 1:13-14

May our Lord Jesus Christ himself and God our Father, who loved us and by his grace gave us eternal encouragement and good hope, encourage your hearts and strengthen you in every good deed and word.
2 Thessalonians 2:16-17

So then, just as you received Christ Jesus as Lord, continue to live in him, rooted and built up in him, strengthened in the faith as you were taught, and overflowing with thankfulness.
Colossians 2:6-7

Pause and Ponder

May we be seekers of His love, vessels hungry to be filled with the beauty of His majesty. Radiate the awe-inspiring glory of our God and live to find ways to walk in the power and splendor of our Almighty God. Salvation is His gift to us; how we live is **our** gift to Him.

From My Heart to Yours

Thank you, Father, for reframing and refocusing my perspective. Today, I will choose to see the following things differently:

_____

_____

_____

_____

_____

_____

_____

_____

_____

_____

_____

_____

_____

_____

_____

_____

_____

_____

_____

_____

_____

God's Best
for Your Life

*D*aughter, I created you to do the good works I planned for you long before I placed you in your mother's womb. As I knit you together perfectly and placed each hair on your head, I knew the tears you would cry, the joy that would swell in your heart, the mountains and obstacles that would challenge you in your faith walk, and the victories that would be yours as My child.

I see your confusion as you approach important crossroads in your life. This testing ground of your faith calls you to go deeper with Me. Cradle My word in your heart and listen for My voice telling you which way to go. Fear will try to take you on a detour from the path I have chosen for you. The easy road looks smooth and beckons you to travel down her highway of deception. The path of least resistance always hold empty promises, for at the end awaits disappointment in a life half-lived and full of "what ifs."

Often the road I have chosen for you looks bumpy and winding so that you cannot see what lies around the next bend. It may be full of mountains and valleys, twists and turns that you are unsure of. But remember, My child, I go before you and make your crooked way straight. I am your rear guard keeping you safe. If you will seek My face and stay close to Me, you will hear My voice tell you when to go to the left or to the right.

Don't miss out on My best for your life—a life well-lived, leaving My imprint on this thirsty world for the hope it needs and found only in Jesus—a life, when finished, will send you smiling as you fly home toward heaven.

The Master Planner and Life Architect,

Your loving Father

Being confident of this, that he who began a good work in you will carry it on to completion until the day of Christ Jesus.
Philippians 1:6

Consider it pure joy, my brothers, whenever you face trials of many kinds, because you know that the testing of your faith develops perseverance. Perseverance must finish its work so that you may be mature and complete, not lacking anything.
James 1:2-4

I will lead the blind by ways they have not known, along unfamiliar paths I will guide them; I will turn the darkness into light before them and make the rough places smooth. These are the things I will do; I will not forsake them.
Isaiah 42:16

Pause and Pray

Father, I praise You for so fearfully and wonderfully creating me with great purpose! My hands I raise in worship, for You are good and Your mercy endures forever. Great and mighty are You, O Lord, and so faithful to complete the good work You began in me from my very beginning. Thank you that the pathway of prayer will always lead me to Your best for my life.

From My Heart to Yours

Today, how will I follow God's plan for my life? What can I do to stay focused on the path He has laid before me?

_____

_____

_____

_____

_____

_____

_____

_____

_____

_____

_____

Wait on God

*L*oved One, I see your tears and hear your cries. I notice the passion burning in your heart to serve Me and run the race fervently and purposefully. You are champing at the bit ready to bolt; instead, you should be at peace resting quietly in My strong arms of trust.

While you may feel ready, I am continually preparing you and others. When I open and fling wide the heavenly gates, all will be in place. While you run, your labor will be fruitful and your harvest ripe.

Wait patiently. Wait with holy anticipation while I am working; the best is yet to come. Keep planning. Keep dreaming. Seek Me! Pursue Me! Ask Me for what you need and desire.

Meditate on My word and bury it deep in your heart. Apply My word to your life, and your faith will swell like a tidal wave, filling you with overflowing hope. Protect your joy—that is your source of strength. Run from strife! Refuse to gossip! Keep your mind pure and reflect on things that are only admirable and lovely.

Release is coming! Until the appointed time, maintain your focus and stay close to Me. Love and bless others every day and keep believing for the impossible. My timing is perfect and I am never late.

Purposefully punctual,

Your loving Father

In my distress I called to the Lord; I cried to my God for help. From his temple he heard my voice; my cry came before him, into his ears.
Psalm 18:6

He lifted me out of the slimy pit, out of the mud and mire; he set my feet on a rock and gave me a firm place to stand. He put a new song in my mouth, a hymn of praise to our God. Many will see and fear and put their trust in the Lord.
Psalm 40:2-3

Whoever gives heed to instruction prospers, and blessed is he who trusts in the Lord.
Proverbs 16:20

Pause and Pray

Father, please forgive me when I get ahead of Your plans. Change my heart and open my eyes fully and completely today. I only want You at the center of my existence. Please give me an undivided heart as I learn to wait patiently so that I may serve You wholeheartedly in all that I do.

From My Heart to Yours

How can I prioritize my day to make room for God's plan?
What am I believing God to do in my life today, next week,
and beyond?

_____

_____

_____

_____

_____

_____

_____

_____

_____

_____

_____

_____

_____

_____

_____

_____

_____

_____

_____

Heaven's Song of Joy

Daughter, may your heart be full of My joy today and overflow with blessed hope. When you are weak, I will strengthen you as you learn to rely solely on Me for your every breath. My right hand will sustain and enable you to stand strong and firm. Abide faithfully in Me and I will abide in you; you will bear much fruit.

Let your heart sing in anticipation of all I am doing in your life. Though your eyes cannot see what I am orchestrating each day, let your faith soar on the wings of hope. Revel in My love, and enjoy every minute of this day. My plans for you are greater than you can possibly imagine, and the love I've woven into them is far beyond your comprehension.

Sing in the shadow of My wings, for I lift you high! Praise Me from a heart full of thankfulness, spilling over with adoring love. Joyfully unwrap the hidden gifts of talents and abilities I selected specifically for you as you trust Me to do a transforming work in your life. Awaken, My child, to the wondrous person I have created you to be. May joy lift you to greater heights as you sing your way throughout this blessed day!

Your life's Orchestral Conductor,

Your loving Father

So do not fear, for I am with you; do not be dismayed, for I am your God. I will strengthen you and help you; I will uphold you with my righteous right hand.
Isaiah 41:10

May the God of hope fill you with all joy and peace as you trust in him, so that you may overflow with hope by the power of the Holy Spirit.
Romans 15:13

Sing praises to God, sing praises; sing praises to our King, sing praises. For God is the King of all the earth; sing to him a psalm of praise.
Psalm 47: 6-7

Pause and Ponder

May your heart be radiant with God's love, overflowing with hope renewed, and singing with heaven's joy untold. For a canopy of glory hovers over all the earth resplendent in the majesty of Almighty God!

From My Heart to Yours

What song is on my heart today? How can I use it to bring glory to my Father?

_____

_____

_____

_____

_____

_____

_____

_____

_____

_____

_____

_____

_____

_____

_____

_____

_____

_____

_____

Grace for Supernatural Peace

*D*aughter, grab hold of My lifeline of hope and hold tight. Never let go as I pull you through the turbulent, stormy waters that are tossing you about on waves of uncertainty and doubt. You will find My peace in the middle of the raging sea where gigantic waves of fear, worry, and unbelief threaten to crash over you and pull you under. Though the waters swell around you and thunder booms its voice of defeat, know that I am always near. My love and grace will surround you like a life jacket, keeping you secure and safe during the storm.

I am your ever-present help in times of trouble. My light shines in the darkness around you, illuminating the promises of My Word. You can overcome any giant who dares to block your path, any weapon formed against you, and any situation that threatens to overtake you. Jesus gave you My perfect peace when He left this world and took His heavenly seat at My right hand as ruler of all. Rest assured, He reigns with the enemy of your soul under His feet.

Cry out the name of Jesus, the name that makes demons tremble and shake—the Name above all names filled with power and authority from on high. You are not alone, My child! Even when you cannot see Me, and when you reach for Me and think I am not there, know in the depth of your heart that I fill the atmosphere around you.

In this world you will have troubles and trials, but take heart and do not give up, for I have overcome this world! Nothing—and I mean nothing—can pluck you from My

93

hand, for you are Mine. I have sealed you with the Holy Spirit and you belong to Me. Know that I work everything out for your good. Christ is exalted in your body as My child—whether by life or by death—for it is written that "to live is Christ and to die is gain." (Phil 1:21 NIV)

Beloved, I am with you. My breath of power is in you. Now, rest under the shelter of My wings and know that I am God, your Yahweh.

Faith overcomes,

Your loving Father

"Peace I leave with you; my peace I give you. I do not give to you as the world gives. Do not let your hearts be troubled and do not be afraid."
John 14:27

May the God of hope fill you with all joy and peace as you trust in Him, so that you may overflow with hope by the power of the Holy Spirit.
Romans 15:13

But now, this is what the LORD says—he who created you, O Jacob, he who formed you, O Israel: "Fear not, for I have redeemed you; I have summoned you by name; you are mine. When you pass through the waters, I will be with you; and when you pass through the rivers, they will not sweep over you. When you walk through the fire, you will not be burned; the flames will not set you ablaze."
Isaiah 43:1-2

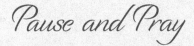

Pause and Pray

Father, when I am weak and afraid, the breath of hope and supernatural peace that is found only in You, makes me strong enough to face any storm. Thank you that You are with me always.

From My Heart to Yours

How will I walk in new mercies and peace today, knowing that my Father is always with me?

_____

_____

_____

_____

_____

_____

_____

_____

_____

_____

_____

_____

_____

Seek God's Shelter

I am the Lord your God. I am your refuge and strength. I go before you, daughter, and pave the way. I am your rear guard that protects you day and night. Do not listen to the misguided words of man. Do not fear or be discouraged by those who speak words contrary to the truth of My Word.

I am the Lord your God, the Creator of this universe. I am the Most High God and when you dwell in My shelter, you will find rest in the shadow of My wings. I am the strong tower you can run to and be safe.

Fear not, My child! Remember whose you are. Remember your worth is found in Me and Me alone. When you accepted my gift of salvation, I sealed you with the Holy Spirit and you became Mine. Every promise in My Word is true. No man can ever take that away from you. No man can diminish your worth as long as you keep your eyes on Me and My truth buried deep in the fertile soil of your heart and mind.

When you abide in Me and I abide in you, when your life is intimately woven together with Mine, when I am the constant in your life you cling to, as it is written, then no harm will befall you and no disaster will come near your tent that I cannot overcome. I command My mighty warrior angels to watch over you, lift you up, and keep you safe.

Come rest in the shadow of My wings and believe in My promises. I am with you, for you, and will never leave you. Look up and fix your eyes on Me and do not waiver. My everlasting love holds you close and secure. You belong to Me.

Defender and Protector,

Your loving Father

The Lord is my rock, my fortress and my deliverer; my God is my rock, in whom I take refuge. He is my shield and the horn of my salvation, my stronghold. I call to the Lord, who is worthy of praise, and I am saved from my enemies.
Psalm 18:2-3

But you will not leave in haste or go in flight; for the Lord will go before you, the God of Israel will be your rear guard.
Isaiah 52:12

He who dwells in the shelter of the Most High will rest in the shadow of the Almighty. I will say of the Lord, "He is my refuge and my fortress, my God, in whom I trust."
Psalm 91:1-2

Pause and Pray

Father, I am thankful that You, and You alone, are my refuge and strength. It is Your right hand that sustains and holds me close. Abba Father, I want You first in my life today and always. Please heighten my sensitivity to the Holy Spirit, give me Your wisdom, and grant me the strength I need to serve You in greater ways. My heart is Yours.

From My Heart to Yours

Lord, I open my heart and mind to You. Today, Your promises have shown me the following:

_____

_____

_____

_____

_____

_____

_____

_____

_____

_____

_____

_____

_____

Sow Seeds in Faith

*B*eloved, you come before Me with a heavy heart full of questions. Do not judge what you do not know. You cannot see the ways I am moving. You cannot see or possibly comprehend how I am going ahead of you and planning your future.

To the human eye you see failure, questioning whether you should carry on. What do you know? Every seed you plant goes forth in many directions. You plant the seed, I make the seed grow, and harvesters are waiting to gather what you've planted. You cannot and will not see any of this.

Sow in faith. Keep planting My seeds of love into the hearts I put before you. Rest in My sovereign will knowing that I have it all covered. The work is not easy, but you toil not in vain. You will reap a harvest if you do not give up.

How I long for you to rest in the stillness and comfort of trusting in Me! Let go of analyzing everything that happens. You are looking through eyes that are limited to your circumstances. I see the possibilities, the path I've set before you, and the end that I've known from the beginning.

Praise Me in the little and praise Me in the abundance. Fill the heavens with your worship from a heart spilling over with love and adoration for Me. Plant your seeds as I lead you and have faith that your harvest is coming!

The Master Gardener,

Your loving Father

*I planted the seed, Apollos watered it, but God
made it grow. So neither he who plants nor he
who waters is anything, but only
God, who makes things grow.*
1 Corinthians 3:6-7

*Let us not become weary in doing good,
for at the proper time we will reap a
harvest if we do not give up.*
Galatians 6:9

*Because your love is better than life, my lips will
glorify you. I will praise you as long as I live, and
in your name I will lift up my hands.*
Psalm 63:3-4

Pause and Ponder

Put the little you have into God's mighty hands and He will
multiply it. But first, give thanks and praise God for the
miracle as if it has already happened. Faithfully plant seeds
that will one day bear fruit from here to eternity.

From My Heart to Yours

Lord, today I submit my seedlings to You, trusting that You will cause them to grow. I am believing You for increase and a harvest in these areas of my life:

_____

_____

_____

_____

_____

_____

_____

_____

_____

_____

_____

_____

_____

_____

_____

_____

_____

_____

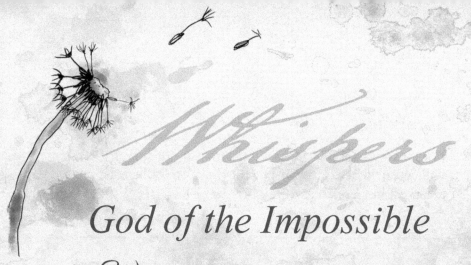

God of the Impossible

What is man that you are mindful of him? What can man do that I cannot? Your hope is not in what a person can do for you. Your hope is in Me, the Creator of all things!

Man can only see the finite things. I see into eternity. **I** know the end from the beginning. ***I AM*** the One that shuts the mouths of lions, walls up the Red Sea, and raises dry bones into a vast army. Man is limited, but **I** am limitless!

Flex your faith muscles when man tries to squelch your dreams. Remember My words when defeat dares to knock on your door. I am God of the impossible and I hold the key to this universe. What is man that you are mindful of him? Place your complete trust into My capable hands. Ride on My wings of faith and do not bend when winds of doubt and unbelief blow. Stand tall and I will hold you firm under the hurricane force of uncertainty that tries to flatten you.

Rise tall, My child, and let your faith soar to new heights. I hold you in My hand, and I am in control. What is man that you are mindful of him? Lean on, trust in, and believe the One through Whom all things are possible. The good work I have begun in you will be finished.

Lifting you up,

Your loving Father

So we say with confidence, "The Lord is my helper; I will not be afraid. What can man do to me?"
Hebrews 13:6

Jesus replied, "What is impossible with men is possible with God."
Luke 18:27

He gives strength to the weary and increases the power of the weak. Even youths grow tired and weary, and young men stumble and fall; but those who hope in the LORD will renew their strength. They will soar on wings like eagles; they will run and not grow weary, they will walk and not be faint.
Isaiah 40:29-31

Pause and Ponder

As you eat from the daily table of life, you are often handed smelly dishes piled high with trials pungent with the unpleasant odors of failure and disappointment. When life dishes out smelly circumstances, find the glory in it and serve back the Heavenly aroma of hope and redeemed suffering. Rejoice that you serve the God of the impossible!

From My Heart to Yours

Despite the challenges today may bring, how can I trust God to intervene on my behalf? What can I do today to serve Him with an attitude of hope?

_____

_____

_____

_____

_____

_____

_____

_____

_____

_____

_____

_____

_____

_____

_____

_____

_____

_____

_____

A Day of Promise

As the warmth of the dawn's early rays caress your face, as the cheerful chatter of the bird's morning song light up your heart, count your blessings and rejoice in this new day I've given you.

Each day is full of promise, a blank page in your life story waiting to be written. Which words will define your experience as the fiery setting sun brings the day's opportunities to a close? Will your page of life be written as a beautiful poem reflecting the love you shared, the lives you touched, or the difference you made? Or will your page have scratches written on it that say frustrated, angry, unforgiving, and dissatisfied?

Loved One, I bring you fresh beginnings each day and the choice is yours whether to look for the beauty within it or the disappointment of another day not meeting up to your tarnished expectations.

Turn your heart to Me, child, and choose to live in the circle of My will instead of your own self-centered will. When you are within My perfect will for your life, it changes the color of your world completely. Everything looks brighter with the softness of hope and brilliant with unimaginable joy. When you chase the desires of your flesh, skies turn from sunny to cloudy to the blackest of storms. Chaos, anxiety, and worry become the tormentors of your day when you choose this way of life.

The page of this new day yearns to be written. Follow Me and walk hand in hand with the One who longs to guide your every step into a life of purpose, of joy, and untold beauty.

The Author and Finisher of your faith,

Your loving father

This is the day the Lord has made; let us rejoice and be glad in it.
Psalm 118:24

Because of the Lord's great love we are not consumed, for his compassions never fail. They are new every morning; great is your faithfulness.
Lamentations 3:22-23

I will sprinkle clean water on you, and you will be clean; I will cleanse you from all your impurities and from all your idols. I will give you a new heart and put a new spirit in you; I will remove from you your heart of stone and give you a heart of flesh. And I will put my Spirit in you and move you to follow my decrees and be careful to keep my laws.
Ezekiel 36:25-27

Pause and Ponder

When your day is a treasure hunt for God's glory, the prize you will capture is joy! May your capacity to see the love gifts God has given you enhance the glorious experience of uncovering His matchless wonders of life with the miracle of hope.

From My Heart to Yours

What words do I want my life to reflect and fill today's page?

_____

_____

_____

_____

_____

_____

_____

_____

_____

_____

_____

_____

_____

Whispers

Walk
Secure and Confident

*Y*ou have been redeemed. You are a blood-bought child of God. I have fearfully and wonderfully designed you to be who you are. Do not compare yourself to others. Be confident in your abilities, knowing it is I who gives them to you. Let words of life pour from your heart and mouth, not words that belittle yourself. That is offensive! Your security lies in Me, not in anyone nor any**thing** in this world. I created you with a great purpose. I am stretching you, teaching you, and preparing you to walk the path I created. For whom much is given, much is required.

Don't question. Seek Me and you will find Me. Open your eyes and see what is right before you. I am here! Call out My name and I will answer. Humility of heart and total surrender of yourself is required. Now get up, look up, and let your faith rise and soar. I AM THE LORD YOUR GOD AND YOU ARE MINE! Look to Me and your heart's desires will be so. Though you stumble, you will not fall. You may bend, but you will not break.

Forever and always,

Your loving Father

In him we have redemption through his blood, the forgiveness of sins, in accordance with the riches of God's grace that he lavished on us with all wisdom and understanding.
Ephesians 1:7-8

Let us fix our eyes on Jesus, the author and perfecter of our faith, who for the joy set before him endured the cross, scorning its shame, and sat down at the right hand of the throne of God.
Hebrews 12:2

The tongue has the power of life and death, and those who love it will eat its fruit.
Proverbs 18:21

Pause and Ponder

Fill the empty pages of your life with the color of God's grace, your ink strokes with hope, and your redeemed story with God's glory. What will you write on the tablet of your heart today?

From My Heart to Yours

Father, today I will walk in a new level of confidence. What steps can I take to walk it out in my job, with my relationships, etc.?

_____
_____
_____
_____
_____
_____
_____
_____
_____
_____
_____
_____
_____
_____
_____
_____
_____
_____

Pray Anyway

*Y*ou have become silent, precious one, and I miss our daily time of communion. Let not the circumstances around you—no matter how dire they may seem—keep you from Me. Pray anyway!

Though it may appear (and you may feel) that I am far away, pray anyway. Hope deferred makes the heart sick. When you pray anyway, My grace fills your spirit with faith so that hope rises once again to give you wings.

Prayer ushers you into My presence. When you are on your knees, your heart cry reaches My throne room of grace and My power is released to meet every need.

Come boldly before Me with your petitions. Know that when you pray and make requests according to My will, I will hear you. When I hear your faith-filled voice, you will have what you have asked of Me.

Your simple yet travailing prayers can and will move mountains. Ask boldly with no limitations. I am God and nothing is impossible with Me. I know your every need before it spills forth from your lips.

Prayer connects you to Me—your lifeline and ever-present help in times of trouble and times of great joy. I long for your fellowship, daughter. Lift your eyes to the heavens from where your help comes from. When you think you can't, pray anyway. I am waiting for you.

Waiting in the secret places,

Your loving Father

*Be joyful in hope, patient in affliction,
faithful in prayer.*
Romans 12:12

*This is the confidence we have in approaching
God: that if we ask anything according to his will,
he hears us. And if we know that he hears
us—whatever we ask—we know that we
have what we asked of him.*
1 John 5:14-15

*God is our refuge and strength, an
ever-present help in trouble.*
Psalm 46:1

Pause and Pray

Father, You are bigger than any problem, circumstance, or roadblock I face. Your whisper of grace quiets the world's frenzy within my soul. I am so thankful that Your promises don't have expiration dates and neither do my prayers. Help me persevere faithfully in prayer even when I don't feel that I can. May Your grace fall like rain on my thirsty soul and soak my spirit with ever-rising faith. Only You can mend the tattered wings of my heart so I can fly with the eagles once again.

From My Heart to Yours

Father, today I bring You my prayers and petitions knowing that You will meet my needs. These are the things weighing on my heart and mind:

_____

_____

_____

_____

_____

_____

_____

_____

_____

_____

_____

_____

_____

_____

_____

_____

_____

_____

Refined to Shine

Have peace, My child. Do not become overwhelmed by what is happening around you and in you. I am preparing you for the work I planned for you from the beginning. This period of refining is necessary to purge you of anything hindering you from My presence. Repent of your sins. Spend time reflecting on your life, your motives, and your thoughts. I am bringing to your mind things long-hidden that need to be exposed to the light so you can be thoroughly cleansed. I will open your eyes to My truth so you can see things as I see them. My Spirit will empower you, comfort you, and reveal things you have never understood before. It is a cleansing process; while it may be painful, know that I am with you every step of the way.

When you have passed through the fire, you will be ready for all I have prepared. Yield completely to Me and keep My Word close to your heart. My hand is upon you and you are Mine. Open yourself to Me wholeheartedly so I can pour out My love through you.

Burn brightly, My child, and let My light illuminate your being for all to see.

The Mender of your soul,

Your loving father

*Therefore judge nothing before the appointed
time; wait till the Lord comes. He will bring to
light what is hidden in darkness and will
expose the motives of the heart.*
1 Corinthians 4:5

*To the Jews who had believed him, Jesus said,
"If you hold to my teaching, you are really my
disciples. Then you will know the truth,
and the truth will set you free."*
John 8:31-32

*"You are the light of the world. A city on a
hill cannot be hidden. Neither do people light a
lamp and put it under a bowl. Instead they put it
on its stand, and it gives light to everyone in the
house. In the same way, let your light shine before
others, that they may see your good deeds and
glorify your Father in heaven."*
Matthew 5:14-16

Pause and Ponder

Sometimes the season we are in is just plain tough! When the
heat of trials or adversity intensifies, search your heart and
ask the Holy Spirit what He is trying to teach you. Instead of
complaining about your troubles, allow Wisdom and Truth
to complete their work in you, and become a more effective
vessel God can use to bless others.

From My Heart to Yours

What is the Father revealing to me that needs to be purged from my life? How can I take action to remove these things? How will it change my perspective and my life?

_____

_____

_____

_____

_____

_____

_____

_____

_____

_____

_____

_____

_____

_____

_____

_____

_____

Whispers

Scales of Justice and Mercy

*C*onduct your affairs with justice. In all you do, walk with the utmost integrity. Let your steps be filled with honor and strength in My righteousness.

You are a light in this world consumed with the darkness of deceit, slimy pits of death and destruction, and deep caverns of greed and selfishness. How you conduct your affairs matters. You are My witnesses and ambassadors of Heaven's Kingdom—the eyes of the world see every move you make.

The heat of temptation grows hotter as the enemy turns up the furnace of his fiery lies by placing ever-subtle traps of deception along your path. How you live your life matters more than you know.

Submit yourself unto Me. Resist the enemy of your soul and he will flee. I will always provide a way out of temptation's luring doorway of death if you will set your mind to walk in My commands and live a life of righteousness.

Let justice and mercy be the scales weighing every decision you make. Let the light of My truth burn in your heart; a fire disintegrating all that is impure. My people cannot look, talk, and act like the world then expect My favor and blessings to pour over them.

Wash in My streams of mercy. Bathe in the river of forgiveness. Be cleansed from the grime of this world's filthy ways. The healing waters of grace make all things new. Rise up and step forth fully clothed in humility and righteousness that is yours by the precious blood of Jesus. Let your life be a testimony to the wasteland of hungry souls searching for hope in the darkness that covers this world.

May justice, mercy, and grace govern your every step. Your actions speak louder than any words you can ever say.

Receive My grace and mercy,

Your loving Father

Good will come to him who is generous and lends freely, who conducts his affairs with justice. Surely he will never be shaken; a righteous man will be remembered forever.
Psalm 112:5-6

Righteousness guards the man of integrity, but wickedness overthrows the sinner.
Proverbs 13:6

When tempted, no one should say, "God is tempting me." For God cannot be tempted by evil, nor does he tempt anyone; but each one is tempted when, by his own evil desire, he is dragged away and enticed. Then, after desire has conceived, it gives birth to sin; and sin, when it is full-grown, gives birth to death.
James 1:13-15

Pause and Ponder

Don't let your sparkle get tarnished by the slime of the world and its ways. Polish and shine your heart daily with the word of God to keep the glitter and glow of Jesus bright and shiny for all to see. Freely forgive and speak encouraging words of life as you influence others for Jesus today.

From My Heart to Yours

How may my words and actions bless or serve someone today?

_____

_____

_____

_____

_____

_____

_____

_____

_____

_____

_____

_____

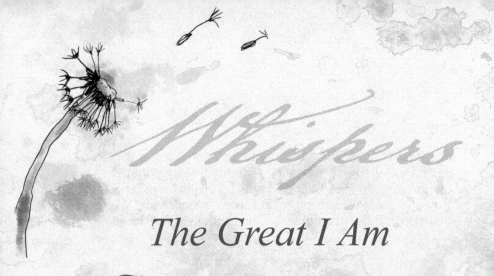

The Great I Am

I **AM** with you everywhere you go. Look for Me in the endless sky above that stretches as far as the east is to the west.

I **AM** with you as you walk in the brilliant light of the sun as it washes over you, bathing you in warmth.

I **AM** with you when gentle breezes blow softly across your face in a caress of grace.

I **AM** the Creator of the birds that sing a symphony of morning cheer, welcoming you into a new day made just for you—a day of new beginnings and fresh starts.

I **AM** the master Gardener of the flowers that blossom and blanket the earth with magnificent color.

I **AM** reflected in the person who shares a smile or compliment with you at the right moment or in a sermon that speaks directly to your heart when hungry for My word.

I **AM** with you as you enjoy the gentle lapping of the ocean waves so deep and wide.

I **AM** the master Painter of the fiery sunset, ablaze with streaks of amber, silver and gold—a stunning display of My glory that takes your breath away.

I **AM** the One who breathes life and hope into your darkness. Worry and doubt may stoke your fears, but as you lean into My dependable and loving arms, I draw you closer still, for **I AM** ever near. Let go, My child, and walk steadily in My grace, seeking always My truth and My face.

I AM the Lord your God; My love for you knows no bounds. Forever endless, forevermore.

All that I AM,

Your loving Father

> "*B*lessed be your glorious name, and may it be exalted above all blessing and praise. You alone are the LORD. You made the heavens, even the highest heavens, and all their starry host, the earth and all that is on it, the seas and all that is in them. You give life to everything, and the multitudes of heaven worship you."
> Nehemiah 9:5-6

> *D*o you not know? Have you not heard? The LORD is the everlasting God, the Creator of the ends of the earth. He will not grow tired or weary, and his understanding no one can fathom.
> Isaiah 40:28

> *W*e wait in hope for the LORD; he is our help and our shield. In him our hearts rejoice, for we trust in his holy name.
> Psalm 33: 20-21

Pause and Pray

Father, my heart is overwhelmed with thankfulness for all that You are! No matter where I am, all I have to do is open my eyes and I will see You. Your presence fills me with hope, strengthens me when I am weak, and comforts me always. With all of my heart I praise You, my Yahweh!

From My Heart to Yours

With renewed faith and awe for who You are, I realize who I am and why I am here. Because of who You are, I know that I am the following:

I am _____

_____

I am _____

_____

I am _____

_____

I am _____

_____

I am _____

_____

Walk the Divine Path

*D*aughter, follow closely in My footsteps. The path I've carved out for you, only you, is full of treasures waiting to be discovered. You must, however, be faithful to listen to My voice. Use My wisdom and discernment in your choices and carefully take each step I mapped out for you. Be alert and fully present at each divine intersection strategically set up for you.

My child, set your mind on living each day for eternity: living to bless others, full of kindness, exploding with joy and a never-ending supply of grace and forgiveness.

Oh, the heavenly path that stretches before you is full of promise! Walk with Me, hand in hand, and discover the glorious riches of your inheritance in Christ Jesus right here, right now.

Unlimited possibilities stretch as far as the eye can see. Choose this day to look through the lenses of heaven, and choose wisely the divine path before you. Together, you and I will blaze a forever trail for others to follow that will bring them into My presence for eternity.

A Light for the path ahead,

Your loving Father

The path of the righteous is level; O upright One,
you make the way of the righteous smooth.
Isaiah 26:7

Set your mind on things above, not
on earthly things.
Colossians 3:2

I keep asking that the God of our Lord Jesus
Christ, the glorious Father, may give you the
spirit of wisdom and revelation, so that you may
know him better. I pray also that the eyes of your
heart may be enlightened in order that you may
know the hope to which he has called you, the
riches of his glorious inheritance in the
saints, and his incomparably great
power for us who believe.
Ephesians 1:17-19

Pause and Ponder

While your eyes cannot see past the bend in the road, God sees, and He knows exactly what lies ahead. Trust God with the highway of your life. He will guide you to each turn, each stop and each fork along the way. Elohim is the GPS that will bring you to your eternal destination right on time.

From My Heart to Yours

How will I use God's encouragement to guide and direct my path today?

_____

_____

_____

_____

_____

_____

_____

_____

_____

_____

_____

_____

_____

_____

_____

_____

_____

_____

_____

_____

_____

Speak to Dry Bones

I am stretching you. I am taking you outside of what is known so your faith will take you into the unknown where complete dependency and trust in Me is essential. My children live in the supernatural realm and not by the world's standards. Believe, only believe, and live each day by faith and by what is not seen.

Let go of your constant questions of "why." Allow Me to do a work in you so you can move forward. The longer you resist, and the longer you try to control, the longer you will stay right where you are.

Greet each day with joy in your heart. Let praise and thanksgiving flow from your lips and speak life into that which I've entrusted to you. I am using you to build faith in others. Learn, grow, and trust in Me. Live each day with gladness and love in your heart. Walk out the vision I have birthed in you and continue to dream with Me.

My timing is perfect. While you cannot see how I am working, *believe* that I am. Good things come to those who wait upon Me. Raise your level of expectation and speak to the dry bones of your dream. They will arise as a mighty army and ultimately victory will resound in your tent. Fan the flame of your desire with My Word and as you do, may joy fill your heart to overflowing!

Rise up in faith,

Your loving Father

For though we live in the world, we do not wage war as the world does.
2 Corinthians 10:3

Through Jesus, therefore, let us continually offer to God a sacrifice of praise—the fruit of lips that confess his name. And do not forget to do good and to share with others, for with such sacrifices God is pleased.
Hebrews 13:15-16

Then he said to me, "Prophesy to these bones and say to them, 'Dry bones, hear the word of the Lord! This is what the Sovereign Lord says to these bones: I will make breath enter you, and you will come to life. I will attach tendons to you and make flesh come upon you and cover you with skin; I will put breath in you, and you will come to life. Then you will know that I am the Lord.'"
Ezekiel 37: 4-6

Pause and Pray

Heavenly Father, thank you for stretching me toward greatness and not leaving me in the trap of going nowhere. How I treasure Your Word that teaches me to take action and speak to the dry bones of my dreams as the prophets and apostles did so many years ago. Raise me up, Lord, to be a pillar standing strong on the Rock of my salvation.

From My Heart to Yours

What dreams do I need to speak into existence today?

_____

_____

_____

_____

_____

_____

_____

_____

_____

_____

_____

_____

_____

_____

_____

_____

_____

_____

Oasis of Change

*D*aughter, I am doing something new. Do not look at the past and mourn the former things. I am the God of fresh beginnings. What I am doing now will not look or feel like the comfortable shoes of yesterday's successes.

Incline your ear, sharpen your gaze, and be alert to My new direction. Moving outside of your comfort zone may be challenging, but if you will remain in Me, seek Me and My Kingdom first, then newness will soon become the anticipation of the here and now.

Live each day with expectant hope that I am working miracles in your life. Only then will your earthly vision sharpen into heaven's vision, clearly revealing My Handprint on all things.

Let go of the old and eagerly embrace the new before you. I am unchanging and ever constant in My love for you; My ways are far greater than anything you can imagine. Your desert is not as dry and barren as you think it is. There's an oasis of life surrounded by fruit-bearing trees and sparkling waters to quench your thirst and sustain your every breath.

Open your eyes and see all that I have for you, child. Succulent fruit to dull pangs of hunger and doubt; refreshing waters of Truth to satisfy your thirsty soul; long, thick branches to shade and protect you from the heat of the battle; and most of all, rest in My presence to recharge and energize you to press on—relentless, joyful, and with great purpose.

Your oasis of change awaits you. Let go of the rusty chains of the past and take hold of today's shiny lifeline that will bring you into tomorrow's destiny and fulfilled promises.

The Fount of Living Water,

Your loving Father

"*F*orget the former things; do not dwell on the past. See, I am doing a new thing! Now it springs up; do you not perceive it? I am making a way in the desert and streams in the wasteland."
Isaiah 43:18-19

*B*ut let all who take refuge in you be glad; let them ever sing for joy. Spread your protection over them, that those who love your name may rejoice in you. For surely, O Lord, you bless the righteous; you surround them with your favor as with a shield.
Psalm 5:11-12

I lift up my eyes to the hills—where does my help come from? My help comes from the Lord, the Maker of heaven and earth.
Psalm 121:1-2

Pause and Ponder

Refuse to live in yesterday's time zone! Resist the urge to fast forward to the light-years of tomorrow. Savor each moment of the gift of this present day. Trust God with all of your tomorrows. Live to glorify God today and, with the rising of each new dawn, rejoice in the love gifts sprinkled throughout the day from your Abba Father.

From My Heart to Yours

Father, forgive me for trying to get ahead of Your plan. I receive Your life-giving Water and take this moment to rest in all that You have done for me. Your Word helps me embrace the change(s) in my life in the following way(s):

_____

_____

_____

_____

_____

_____

_____

_____

_____

_____

_____

_____

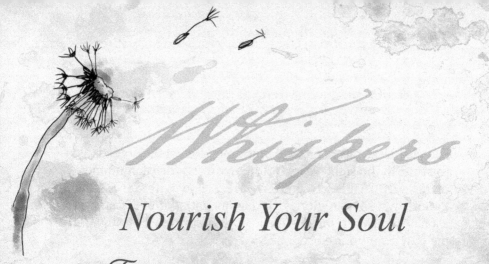

Nourish Your Soul

I am the Way, the Truth, and the Life. I am the required nourishment to sustain you in this world so determined to weigh you down in disillusionment and despair.

Dive into My Word and search for Me with all of your heart. I will unlock treasures within My Word as you diligently seek to know Me. Day by day, I will enlighten the eyes of your heart and bring understanding to your soul as Wisdom reveals the mysteries I long for you to discover through the inspired pages of My timeless book of love.

As My dearly loved child, you must deny yourself and pick up your cross and follow Me if you want total victory in your life. Allow My truth to sink into the very depths of your soul so you can fully understand Me and run your race victoriously.

Do not allow the enemy to sit at your table! Watch out for Satan's strategically placed lies and deceptions seeking to derail you along your journey. Constantly guard against busyness, unbelief, and weariness. In Me, you have everything you need to overcome all things. Feast on the essential food for your soul found only in My life-giving Word.

Stay the course. Find joy, peace, and contentment each day on the way toward tomorrow. Refuse to give in or give up! Those who persevere will reach their Promise Land. Keep your eyes fixed on Me and obey all of My commands.

The Source of life,

Your loving Father

I keep asking that the God of our Lord Jesus Christ, the glorious Father, may give you the Spirit of wisdom and revelation, so that you may know him better. I pray also that the eyes of your heart may be enlightened in order that you may know the hope to which he has called you, the riches of his glorious inheritance in the saints, and his incomparably great power for us who believe.
Ephesians 1:17-19

I wait for the Lord, my soul waits, and in his word I put my hope.
Psalm 130:5

Blessed is the man who perseveres under trial, because when he has stood the test, he will receive the crown of life that God has promised to those who love him.
James 1:12

Pause and Ponder

Today's moments are sparkling jewels in life's treasure chest of memories. Enjoy the here and now like never before! Don't get derailed by distraction. Fix your gaze on high and follow the footsteps of Jesus.

From My Heart to Yours

Lord, am I getting my daily nourishment from You or from the world? Thank you for opening my eyes to the following:

_____

_____

_____

_____

_____

_____

_____

_____

_____

_____

_____

_____

_____

_____

_____

_____

_____

_____

Dream Big with God

Do you hear My voice? I am planting desires in your heart to fulfill what I have called you to do. Do not allow the greatness of what I ask to overwhelm you. I am in control and will work out each detail to accomplish the purpose for your life.

Dare to dream . . . and dream BIG! You serve a mighty God! Trust Me and have mountain moving faith to believe that, with Me, what seems impossible is not. Let go . . . turn all that you are over to Me so I can purify and mold you into the intricately sculpted masterpiece I created you to be. A bold witness, in My image and likeness, ready to do the good works I planned for your life.

Greater things await, so look up **expectantly** for all you need. Enjoy the journey and keep watch for what I am doing. Be careful to obey all that I command and you will move toward your destiny. Cease trying to figure out how things will happen because only I know these things.

Stay on course and let your love for others increase and overflow. There is much to do. Rejoice! Be glad! Let My hope fill your heart and flow like a waterfall.

The Alpha and the Omega,

Your loving Father

May he give you the desire of your heart and make all your plans succeed.
Psalm 20:4

He replied, "Because you have so little faith. I tell you the truth, if you have faith as small as a mustard seed, you can say to this mountain, 'Move from here to there' and it will move. Nothing will be impossible for you."
Matthew 17:20-21

May the Lord make your love increase and overflow for each other and for everyone else, just as ours does for you.
1 Thessalonians 3:12

Pause and Ponder

May God be the light that leads your heart and directs your footsteps to the dreams and desires He has specially planned for you. Dream big and don't put limitations on yourself. For with God, all things really are possible. The future is a question mark full of His promises.

From My Heart to Yours

I am ready to take the limits off of myself and dream BIG!
My list of big dreams:

_____

_____

_____

_____

_____

_____

_____

_____

_____

_____

_____

_____

_____

_____

_____

_____

_____

_____

_____

_____

_____

Stand and Fight

*B*e still, child, and quiet your frenzied soul. Rest in My presence and let My peace saturate every part of you. Lay all of your burdens at My feet and leave them there. You were never meant to carry such heavy burdens! Cast your anxieties on Me and trust Me with your all.

It is time for you to pick up the spiritual weapons I have given you and fight off the attacks of the enemy. Recognize the enemy's cunning tactics as he shoots arrows of doubt, worry, fear, and anxiety at your weakest points. Deflect those arrows with My Word and declare that you are more than a conqueror; where you are weak, I make you strong. Proclaim the battle is already won—no weapon or plan formed against you shall prosper in the name of Jesus!

Stand on My Word and fight. Refuse to allow doubt and worry tear down your wall of faith and belief. You are My child and you are sealed with the Holy Spirit. Get up and fight for victory is near.

The battle will heat up but fear not, for I am with you. Cast off all that binds you and walk in My freedom and peace. My grace gifts are yours through the shed blood of your Savior, Jesus. Rest in My presence and be filled with the power of My Spirit. Together we will see it through to victory.

Walk boldly today,

Your loving Father

"Come to me, all you who are weary and burdened, and I will give you rest. Take my yoke upon you and learn from me, for I am gentle and humble in heart, and you will find rest for your souls. For my yoke is easy and my burden is light."
Matthew 11:28-30

Finally, be strong in the Lord and in his mighty power. Put on the full armor of God so that you can take your stand against the devil's schemes.
Ephesians 6:10-11

It is God who arms me with strength and makes my way perfect. He makes my feet like the feet of a deer; he enables me to stand on the heights. He trains my hands for battle; my arms can bend a bow of bronze. You give me your shield of victory; you stoop down to make me great. You broaden the path beneath me, so that my ankles do not turn.
2 Samuel 22:33-37

Pause and Ponder

When pricked by fear and pounded with lies, send the enemy of your soul tumbling by speaking aloud the Living Word that is sharper than any double-edged sword. May each trial, each loss and, each victory drum the notes of your life into a heart song of worship to Almighty God.

From My Heart to Yours

What do you need to stand and fight for today?

_____
_____
_____
_____
_____
_____
_____
_____
_____
_____
_____
_____
_____
_____
_____
_____
_____
_____
_____
_____
_____
_____

Lay Down Your Life

Drink deeply from My cup, child, that overflows with love, favor, and blessings. With this cup comes sacrifice. Are you willing to sacrifice so that you can walk in the fullness of all I have for you? The way is not easy, but it is full of great promise, victory, and joy. You must, however, lose yourself before you can find who you are in Me.

Bring all of yourself to My altar and lay it down. Be cleansed by the precious blood of My Son who died to give you forgiveness and freedom from all things. Victory is yours and is already won.

Give Me your all, child, and all I have will be yours. Serve Me with your entire heart and your desires will be satisfied. In Me, all things are perfected. Abide in Me and I will abide in you. Together, we will walk out your journey with purpose and passion. With Me, all things are possible, but you must believe.

Trust in Me,

Your loving Father

Then Jesus said to his disciples, "Whoever wants to be my disciple must deny themselves and take up their cross and follow me. For whoever wants to save his life will lose it, but whoever loses his life for me will find it."
Matthew 16:24-25

"Love the Lord your God with all your heart and with all your soul and with all your mind and with all your strength. The second is this: 'Love your neighbor as yourself.' There is no commandment greater than these."
Mark 12: 30-31

Therefore, I urge you, brothers, in view of God's mercy, to offer your bodies as a living sacrifice, holy and pleasing to God—this is your spiritual act of worship.
Romans 12:1

Pause and Pray

Father, I give You all of me with a heart that is ever thankful for the great love and sacrifice Jesus made to give me new life and forgiveness for all of my sins. I surrender my will to Yours. Fill me with Your abundant love so that I can love others as You love them. All that I am is Yours, Father.

From My Heart to Yours

What do I need to sacrifice in order to completely surrender my will to the Father? What steps or actions can I implement in my daily walk?

_____

_____

_____

_____

_____

_____

_____

_____

_____

_____

_____

_____

_____

_____

_____

_____

_____

_____

_____

Whispers

Beacon of Light

*D*o you hear the cries of the hopeless? When you look into their despairing eyes and see their soul searching for answers, searching for anything that will bring them hope and life, does your heart break with compassion? Do your arms long to comfort the broken? Do your eyes cry tears of righteous anger for the injustice of a world running rampant with evil and deceptive traps?

Daughter, listen closely as I whisper My love into your heart, awakening the call on your life. As you search for Me, My mercy is new with the dawn of each day. It is the key that unlocks the treasure chest of My love revealing the mysteries of Truth that will keep you grounded as you step onto the path set before you. Sparkle with joy. Shine with the brilliance of My love that draws others to My incredible gems of grace, forgiveness, and restoration.

Be a beacon of light that brings the downtrodden to the foot of the cross where new life, restored life, eternal life is eagerly waiting. The resurrection power of My Spirit is within you. Charge forth in holy boldness today with eyes and heart open to the opportunities around you to sow My seeds of love into souls desperate for change—desperate for Me. I will position you to reach people in unexpected places. Be the extension of My open arms of love to gather the lost and bring them to the Savior, the Redeemer, My Son, King Jesus. The harvest is plenty but the workers are few. Answer My call and help bring My lost sheep home.

The Light within,

Your loving Father

"*I*n the same way, let your light shine before
men, that they may see your
good deeds and praise your
Father in heaven."
Matthew 5:16

*W*hen he saw the crowds, he had compassion on
them, because they were harassed and helpless,
like sheep without a shepherd. Then he said to
his disciples, "The harvest is plentiful but the
workers are few. Ask the Lord of the harvest,
therefore, to send out workers
into his harvest field."
Matthew 9:36-38

"*W*hat do you think? If a man owns a hundred
sheep, and one of them wanders away, will he not
leave the ninety-nine on the hills and go to look
for the one that wandered off? And if he finds
it, I tell you the truth, he is happier about that
one sheep than about the ninety-nine that did
not wander off. In the same way your Father in
heaven is not willing that any of these
little ones should be lost."
Matthew 18:12-14

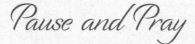

Pause and Pray

Father, I am ready to be a mighty witness for You and, a bright light piercing the darkness in this world so others can find their way toward You. May my heart reflect the beauty of Your love for this broken world in need of Your touch. Give me grace and courage when you tap on my heart asking me to put love into action. When others look at me, Father, may they see You.

From My Heart to Yours

My Father, I want to be a beacon of hope in my community and find Your lost sheep. Who can I approach to offer my time and service on a weekly/monthly basis? I will reach out to the following people/groups:

_____

_____

_____

_____

_____

_____

_____

_____

_____

_____

_____

Run Into His Open Arms of Love

*P*recious daughter of Mine, how I long for you to believe the truth of how great My love is for you. Run into My arms that are open, longing to hold you and wrap you in My love. No valley is too wide, no ocean is too deep, no sin is too great for Me to reach you and rescue your broken and wounded heart.

I am the God who heals and restores. I am the God who cleanses you from all of your sins. Fear not, My child! Let go of *all* that hinders you. Cast off the web of lies woven throughout the fertile soil of your heart like vines, choking out My voice and My love.

I am your gracious and loving Father. I am calling your name! Turn away from all that separates you from Me, and I will sweep in like a mighty rushing wind to catch you as you surrender everything to Me. I will wipe away every tear. I will bathe you in My grace, restoring your grey and battered heart from the storms you have weathered for so long. I will fill you with joy and your hope will soar like the eagles as you are renewed by My love, peace, and supernatural strength.

My vast mercy and grace will cover you like fresh morning dew. I made you perfectly in My image and likeness—a rare beauty to behold. When I look at you, I see a righteous and pure woman of God clothed in the redeeming blood of your Savior, Jesus.

Before you ever came to be, My plans for you were intricately woven into every fiber of who I destined you to be—a beautiful flower shining bright with My love, full of compassion and a heart to serve others. I created you with a purpose that only you can fill.

You have a race to run and, in My strength, you can run victoriously to the end. I am with you always and will never leave you nor forsake you. I am drawing you in, My child. Will you come? Will you run into My outstretched arms that long to hold you close and restore you completely?

In Me you are whole,

Your loving Father

> *For as high as the heavens are above the earth, so great is his love for those who fear him; as far as the east is from the west, so far has he removed our transgressions from us.*
> Psalm 103: 11-12
>
> *"For I know the plans I have for you," declares the Lord, "plans to prosper you and not to harm you, plans to give you hope and a future."*
> Jeremiah 29:11
>
> *Therefore, since we are surrounded by such a great cloud of witnesses, let us throw off everything that hinders and the sin that so easily entangles, and let us run with perseverance the race marked out for us.*
> Hebrews 12:1

Pause and Pray

Thank you, Father, that You love me through every trial and circumstance throughout this journey of my life. I treasure Your peace that is always with me in every moment of need. I praise You for making me a beautifully woven tapestry of Your love, stitched together with great purpose and beauty, so that I may glorify Your name.

From My Heart to Yours

What is hindering me from completely surrendering my will to the Father? What steps can I take to boldly trust Him with my future?

_____

_____

_____

_____

_____

_____

_____

_____

_____

_____

_____

_____

_____

Miracle of Hope

*O*pen wide the doors of your heart and give Me full access to every part of your life. I am not satisfied with only the pieces you choose to dole out to Me. That is offensive! I long to work through you as My vessel to touch and impact others. You must, however, surrender every facet of your being to Me.

When you hold on to the control of your life, you are lengthening the time it takes to accomplish the vision I have set before you. Wake up to this truth and run with Me in total surrender. As you let go and trust Me completely, the weight of worry and anxiety will fall away like chains tumbling to the ground in a heap of steel rubble. Incredible peace and joy will replace that once dead weight allowing you to move in the freedom My Son, Jesus, died to give you.

Walk with Me and beside Me, My child, but never ahead of Me. Declare victory over yourself, your family, and all those I put in your path. Run this race **with** Me and not in your own might which will availeth nothing. Take My outstretched hand and together let's be the miracle of hope someone is waiting for.

Run fearlessly,

Your loving Father

And now, O Israel, what does the Lord your
God ask of you but to fear the Lord your God,
to walk in all his ways, to love him, to serve the
Lord your God with all your heart and with all
your soul, and to observe the Lord's commands
and decrees that I am giving you
today for your own good?
Deuteronomy 10:12-13

"Whoever finds his life will lose it, and
whoever loses his life for my sake
will find it."
Matthew 10:39

O Israel, put your hope in the Lord, for with the
Lord is unfailing love and with
him is full redemption.
Psalm 130:7

Pause and Ponder

Refuse to be tossed about on waves of doubt and seas of
uncertainty. Trust in the Lord! The tangled nets of our efforts
unfurl and fill to overflowing when we cease living life **our**
way and submit to the authority of **God's** way. Today, serve
others a triple helping of laughter, a cup full of love, and
a heaping spoon of hope with a heart brimming over with
heaven's radiant joy.

From My Heart to Yours

Father, how may I be used to experience joy and share it with others?

_____

_____

_____

_____

_____

_____

_____

_____

_____

_____

_____

_____

_____

_____

_____

_____

_____

_____

_____

_____

_____

_____

Whispers

Life Song of Praise

*B*eloved, what is the music of your life playing? Is it the soft strings of an orchestra in perfect harmony, or the loud strumming of a band that is off-key and chaotic?

Daughter, you do not know the plans I have for you, but I do. They are to prosper you and fill you with My life-giving hope. While you cannot see the divine intersections I have carefully orchestrated for you, they are there. Be mindful to keep yourself as a finely-tuned instrument by meditating on My word every day. When you do, each moment that is played out will synchronize with the plans I have for you—an orchestra that beats on time and in full harmony.

Resist the temptation to march to your own drumbeat. When you get outside of My will, the noise will only be loud and off-key. Sharpen your ears to hear the melody of your life I am playing and stay in rhythm. It is when you are perfectly in sync with Me that the notes ring clear as a bell and soft like a gentle rain falling to water the earth with life.

My daughter, My Beloved, rejoice that every day is a new bar being played to perfection in your life song of praise!

The Master Maestro,

Your loving Father

You have made known to me the path of life; you will fill me with joy in your presence, with eternal pleasures at your right hand.
Psalm 16:11

I rejoice in following your statutes as one rejoices in great riches. I meditate on your precepts and consider your ways. I delight in your decrees; I will not neglect your word.
Psalm 119:14-16

I will sing to the Lord all my life; I will sing praise to my God as long as I live. May my meditation be pleasing to him, as I rejoice in the Lord.
Psalm 104:33-34

Pause and Pray

Father, the echo of Your love is the melody on my lips. You are the joy in my soul that keeps my heart beating. May each trial, each loss, and each victory I go through drum the notes of my life into a heart song of worship to You, Almighty God. And may every note of my life song be a lantern that lights the path to my forever home in heaven with You.

From My Heart to Yours

What is God speaking to my heart, even now?

_____

_____

_____

_____

_____

_____

_____

_____

_____

_____

_____

_____

_____

_____

_____

_____

_____

_____

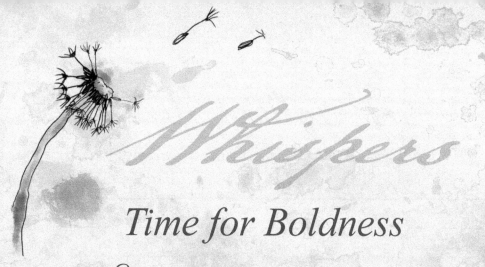

Time for Boldness

Speak the truth of My Word boldly and with confidence. Do not be afraid when I ask you to share My Word with others or confront them in love.

My Word is hidden deep within your heart. Trust the Holy Spirit will bring to remembrance the right words at the right time. No more excuses! No more hiding behind the skirts of fear! Lives are at stake and you are My messenger of light to break through the chains of darkness that bind people in sin and destructive ways.

Immerse yourself in My Word so rivers of living water pour forth from the abundance of your heart. I have called you to be a witness for Me, not a judge. My people cannot turn their heads from the sin running wild and uncontained in My house and this corrupt world controlled by the prince of darkness.

Jesus came to save people from their sin and free them from the bondage of lies that saturate the earth and hold people captive.

If someone were to jump off a cliff, would you look the other way? No, you would not! How much more so should you try to help someone wallowing in sin that keeps them from eternity with Me and throws them into the abyss of flaming hell! Speak and act with love and follow the leadership of the Holy Spirit. Be the bright light of My love that draws people to everlasting life with Me.

The Light in a dark world,

Your loving Father

*Do everything without complaining or arguing
so that you may become blameless and pure,
children of God without fault in a crooked and
depraved generation, in which you shine like
stars in the universe as you hold out the word of
life—in order that I may boast on
the day of Christ that I did not
run or labor for nothing.*
Philippians 2:14-16

*"Do not judge, and you will not be judged. Do
not condemn, and you will not be condemned.
Forgive, and you will be forgiven."*
Luke 6:37

*Instead, speaking the truth in love, we will in
all things grow up into him who is the Head,
that is, Christ. From him the whole body, joined
and held together by every supporting ligament,
grows and builds itself up in love,
as each part does its work.*
Ephesians 4:15-16

Pause and Ponder

Commit to live your life with a holy boldness—a true witness and ambassador of the Most High God. Win people over with God's love that is lived and demonstrated, not just talked about. Jesus died so we could live our lives uncaged and free! May your speech be tempered with gentle words that encourage, and may you always speak the truth in love.

From My Heart to Yours

Father, today I will walk in holy boldness and recognize those You have put in my path. I will pray for/reach out to the following people:

_____

_____

_____

_____

_____

_____

_____

_____

_____

_____

_____

_____

_____

_____

_____

_____

_____

_____

_____

_____

_____

_____

Thirst for God

*A*s the deer pants beside the still water, so should you pant after Me—a thirst that can only be quenched as you drink deeply of My presence every moment of every day. I am a fire that consumes every part of you, not just the parts you choose to give to Me.

I am not an in-between God that is satisfied with only half of your heart. Don't you know that I will spit out of My mouth those who are lukewarm? My love for you is endless and so deep that I gave My most precious gift—My Son—to die so that you may have life, eternal life, and dwell with Me forever.

This world is temporal so beware you do not get caught in the trap of lies and deceit that will blind you from My truth. You cannot serve two masters. I am the one true God. Examine your heart. Search within and repent of any sins that hold you down.

I want all of you. My arms are open and ready for you to run into. Don't tarry—act now! The voice of your Shepherd is calling you.

The Sustainer of Life,

Your loving Father

As the deer pants for streams of water, so my soul pants for you, O God. My soul thirsts for God, for the living God. When can I go and meet with God?
Psalm 42:1-2

"So, because you are lukewarm—neither hot nor cold—I am about to spit you out of my mouth."
Revelation 3:16

So we fix our eyes not on what is seen, but on what is unseen. For what is seen is temporary, but what is unseen is eternal.
2 Corinthians 4:18

Pause and Ponder

Today, lift your eyes to heaven and turn your heart toward the wisdom that comes directly from the throne of God. Fix your hope on Jesus who is the only One who can break the chains of the tyranny of sin and set you free.

From My Heart to Yours

Father, I long to keep my eyes focused on You. Today, I will focus on the following things and submit them to Your will:

_____

_____

_____

_____

_____

_____

_____

_____

_____

_____

_____

_____

_____

_____

_____

_____

_____

_____

_____

_____

Make the Right Choice

I AM HERE! My presence surrounds you wherever you are. In the early morning, the joyous chatter of birds sing My praises as the sun rises to bring forth a new day. Another day to bring Me glory and honor as you walk along the carefully placed stepping stones I have laid out before you.

Opportunities for right choices pepper your path, so I ask . . . what will you choose this day? Will you sacrifice your will and your way and choose My will and My way? Will you humble yourself and allow Me to direct your footsteps that lead to everlasting life? You are an honored vessel of clay with hidden treasures deep within. I long to shape and mold you into My image and likeness; a rare beauty to behold that shines with My resplendent light.

Choose well, precious one. The plans I have for you are beyond anything you can imagine. I will complete My handiwork originally created in you. Take courage, for My plans are to prosper you and never to harm you. In Me awaits abundant life in a land flowing with milk and honey.

Beautiful, redeemed, worthy, and restored are you, My beloved daughter. I am calling you to greater things than you can do on your own. How will you answer?

Walk secure and confident,

Your loving Father

But if serving the Lord seems undesirable to you, then choose for yourselves this day whom you will serve, whether the gods your forefathers served beyond the River, or the gods of the Amorites, in whose land you are living. But as for me and my household, we will serve the Lord.
Joshua 24:15

Yet, O Lord, you are our Father. We are the clay, you are the potter; we are all the work of your hand.
Isaiah 64:8

Therefore, I urge you, brothers, in view of God's mercy, to offer your bodies as living sacrifices, holy and pleasing to God—this is your spiritual act of worship.
Romans 12:1

Pause and Pray

Father, I choose life with You. I offer myself as a living sacrifice to be used for Your glory and Your honor in every area of my life. May Your will be done in my life today.

May the words of my mouth and the meditation of my heart be pleasing in Your sight, O Lord, my Rock and my Redeemer (Psalm 19:14).

From My Heart to Yours

What choices/decisions are set before me that I need to surrender to the Father?

_____

_____

_____

_____

_____

_____

_____

_____

_____

_____

_____

_____

_____

_____

_____

_____

New Life and Purpose

*B*eloved, do you hear Me? Will you respond to My promptings drawing you back to Me? Your feet have strayed from the path I set before you and you've been wandering aimlessly; searching and seeking, but always coming up short.

I am stirring your heart. I am fanning the flames of holy desire in your soul to return to Me. A passion is rising within your heart to know Me intimately, fully surrendered, and humble at heart.

Come into the deep waters of My presence where I will refresh your heavy-laden heart burdened by disappointment and regret. Streams of living water and mercy will flow over you washing away all traces of sin as you seek forgiveness in My arms of love.

Inhale the sweet fragrance of grace rising high above the empty grave of your Savior, Jesus. Sit still and be refreshed as the Holy Spirit breathes life into your hungry heart, satisfying your yearning for something more, something that gives meaning to your very existence. Like the bursting rays of the morning sun, My extravagant love washes warm into every cell of your being bringing new life and purpose to your soul.

A new day has begun; a season of change is before you. I have made all things new. Let your faith soar and your steps be firm as you return to your first love—your Heavenly Father, your All in All.

Sending seasons of refreshment,

Your loving Father

Repent, then, and turn to God, so that your sins may be wiped out, that times of refreshing may come from the Lord.
Acts 3:19

"I desire to do your will, O my God; your law is within my heart."
Psalm 40:8

If you have any encouragement from being united with Christ, if any comfort from his love, if any fellowship with the Spirit, if any tenderness and compassion, then make my joy complete by being like-minded, having the same love, being one in spirit and purpose.
Philippians 2:1-2

Pause and Ponder

Open wide your arms to God's restorative mercy and grace! Take your eyes off yesterday's failures and focus on tomorrow's possibilities. Rise up with resurrection faith that refuses to put a period at the end of disappointment and heartache. Never put a period where God places a comma. God's love never fails!

From My Heart to Yours

What steps can I take to rewrite my story as one that reflects God's love for me? How will my former disappointments be written into new scenes of life?

_____

_____

_____

_____

_____

_____

_____

_____

_____

_____

_____

_____

_____

Whispers

Be a Warrior

As my redeemed born-again child, My life-giving Spirit is within you. My power is in you! Through the blood of Jesus, you are MORE than a conqueror and can overcome ALL things.

Pay close attention to the words that pour out of your mouth. Are they infused with power or laced with defeat? Speak words of power and victory! Child of Mine, I have overcome the world. You have My Spirit and power authorizing you to be victorious in every situation. When you are weak, call out My name and rely on Me to do what you cannot.

My supernatural power is at your fingertips to fight against the enemy of your soul, so use it! Do not accept a mediocre or defeated life. I came that you may have life and life more abundantly. Practice the discipline of lining your words up with the truth of My everlasting Word. When you do this, mountains will move and enemies will fall.

Jesus came to give you life; now, step up and grab hold of what is already yours and walk in total victory. Run your race with power to the very end—super-charged, dynamic, explosive power that belongs to you as My child. Take your stance and forcefully advance My Kingdom. You are able!

Remember Whose you are,

Your loving Father

> *"I have told you these things, so that in me you may have peace. In this world you will have trouble. But take heart! I have overcome the world."*
> John 16:33

> *A wise man's heart guides his mouth, and his lips promote instruction. Pleasant words are a honeycomb, sweet to the soul and healing to the bones.*
> Proverbs 16:23-24

> *"From the days of John the Baptist until now, the kingdom of heaven has been forcefully advancing, and forceful men lay hold of it."*
> Matthew 11:12

Pause and Ponder

Don't allow Satan to poison you with his fiery darts of inadequacy and failure. Stand tall with mountain-moving faith and rise above your disappointments. Pray through your setbacks. Believe God can do the impossible! Fight on your knees, love with His heart, and walk in His truth—always!

From My Heart to Yours

Father, today I will remember that I am more than a conqueror! I will take the following steps and walk in my destiny:

_____

_____

_____

_____

_____

_____

_____

_____

_____

_____

_____

_____

_____

_____

_____

_____

_____

_____

_____

_____

Draw Strength
When Weary

*D*aughter, I know you are weary, drained, and lack the ability to focus. The busyness of this world and expectations of others can overwhelm and close in on you like a thick dark cloud. The sparkle in your life can easily vaporize when despair settles around your shoulders.

Be not discouraged! I am **El Roi** (the God who sees me) and always right here beside you. I fill the very atmosphere you breathe. Come into My presence and let Me fill you, empower you, and renew you. Reconnect with Me by opening your heart to the truth and wisdom found only in My Word. I am your source of power and strength. Keep your gaze steady and your heart true as you travel along the freeway of life. When the speed bumps of opposition come, hold on, for I am right there to steady you amidst the swirling circumstances.

Cast down impure thoughts and run from temptations no matter how minor they may seem. Don't allow even a small opening for your adversary, the devil, to come in and set up a stronghold to keep you in chains. You are in training; excellence in all things is required.

Believe in My promises, speak out declarations of faith, and trust Me. I will not fail you. My throne endures forever. Let My truth settle in your heart to bloom and grow tall. Scatter Your seeds of faith and watch them explode into more than you could ever think or imagine.

The Great Sustainer of life,

Your loving Father

He gives strength to the weary and increases the power of the weak. Even youths grow tired and weary, and young men stumble and fall; but those who hope in the Lord will renew their strength. They will soar on wings like eagles; they will run and not grow weary, they will walk and not be faint.
Isaiah 40: 29-31

But you, man of God, flee from all this, and pursue righteousness, godliness, faith, love, endurance and gentleness. Fight the good fight of the faith. Take hold of the eternal life to which you were called when you made your good confession in the presence of many witnesses.
1 Timothy 6:11-12

Dear children, let us not love with words or tongue but with actions and in truth. This then is how we know that we belong to the truth, and how we set our hearts at rest in his presence whenever our hearts condemn us. For God is greater than our hearts, and he knows everything.
1 John 3:18-20

172

Pause and Ponder

When life careens out of control at speeds like a racecar spinning around that final lap, beware that you don't fall into the deceitful trap of trying to fix your own problems. Instead, choose the quiet confidence of God and grab hold of His hand of trust. Rest in God's provision and wait for the answers to your problems with joyful expectation. As you savor each grace moment with thanks, it will fill your world-weary soul and give you the strength to press on. God never fails!

From My Heart to Yours

Lord, thank you for being an oasis in the desert of life. Today, I will take time to reflect on what Your Word says about the following areas of my life:

_____

_____

_____

_____

_____

_____

_____

_____

_____

_____

Whispers

Crossroads of Decision

*Y*ou are approaching a crossroads, My daughter. The time has come for you to make a choice. You are growing as I stretch you and challenge your faith. Your walk is not easy. Your path is laced with decisions, difficult decisions. That is why you must keep the doors of your heart open to My voice so you can hear Me as I whisper, "This is the way—follow it."

Be receptive to the possibilities I show you. Learn to discern what is for the here and now and what is for the future. My grace is sufficient for you each day. Rely on Me, not yourself, to open the doorway of opportunities that will escalate you into your destiny. What I open no man can shut.

Live your day with joy. Be full of expectation that what I've promised will come to pass. Stay grounded in My Word and My Truth will guide you to make right decisions. Your heart cannot hear Me over the bagpipes of fearful questions playing loudly in your ears. Trust the Holy Spirit to train you how to cast down wrong thoughts immediately. This weapon is honed by meditating on My Word.

I am God, your Father. Listen to Me! Now is not the time to falter in doubt. Take hold of My hand and do not let go. Walk with confidence. Pay no attention to pitfalls that try to block your way. Keep moving. Keep sowing seeds. Keep believing. The best is just ahead!

I believe in you,

Your loving Father

*"These are the words of him who is holy and
true, who holds the key of David. What he
opens no one can shut, and what he
shuts no one can open."*
Revelation 3:7

*We demolish arguments and every pretension
that sets itself up against the knowledge of God,
and we take captive every thought to
make it obedient to Christ.*
2 Corinthians 10:5

*But when you ask, you must believe and not
doubt, because the one who doubts is like a wave
of the sea, blown and tossed by the wind. That
person should not expect to receive anything from
the Lord. Such a person is double-minded
and unstable in all they do.*
James 1:6-7

Pause and Ponder

Step up to your crossroads of decision with confidence that
comes from consistently praying, searching out the Word
of God, and persevering through every trial and hardship
that comes your way. Determination will take you places
you never dreamed you would go. Make it your determined
purpose today to embrace all God has for you!

From My Heart to Yours

What decisions am I facing that have brought me to this crossroad moment? How will I trust the Father today and walk in confidence?

_____

_____

_____

_____

_____

_____

_____

_____

_____

_____

_____

_____

_____

_____

_____

_____

_____

_____

_____

_____

The Heat of Refinement

*A*s you sit in My presence and soak in My love, I am transforming you into a sparkling gem—pure, holy, and lovely. All of the jagged edges are melted and reshaped. With each passing day, each trial, each mountain of opposition you face, know that I am chipping away at the old, dead things in your life so you can move forward in what I have planned and purposed for you.

The process is often painful, and I hear your desperate cries for help. I am here, daughter. Even though your eyes cannot see Me, when it appears I am doing nothing, let your faith arise and believe that I am moving mountains for you.

My Word endures forever and I do not lie. Bow your knee before Me, seek after Me as the truest treasure in your life, and believe with all of your heart that I am working all things out for your good.

Do not despise the broken pieces in your life, for it is there that I work to make you whole. Let not your heart be heavy with sorrow. In your brokenness, My best work is done. I am molding you into a glittering, brilliant jewel—a reflection of My glory, a vessel worthy of sharing My love.

Rejoice, My child, rejoice! The darkness will not hold you down. Joy will burst through in the morning. Believe, only believe.

The Master Potter,

Your loving Father

"*He cuts off every branch in me that bears no fruit, while every branch that does bear fruit he prunes so that it will be even more fruitful.*"
John 15:2

"*The grass withers and the flowers fall, but the word of our God endures forever.*"
Isaiah 40:8

"*And we know that in all things God works for the good of those who love him, who have been called according to his purpose.*"
Romans 8:28

Pause and Pray

Father, I thank you that Your presence is the very air I breathe. You are my hope and the Rock I cling to for my every need. In You, O God, I put my trust . . . today and every day.

From My Heart to Yours

Father, I realize there are things in my life that are holding me back from fulfilling my purpose. Today, I want to surrender these things to You and see Your miraculous hand transform my life:

_____

_____

_____

_____

_____

_____

_____

_____

_____

_____

_____

_____

_____

_____

_____

_____

Whispers

Promised Land Living

$\mathcal{I}$ am the Lord your God. There is no one besides Me. I AM the Way, the Truth, and the Life. Consecrate yourself to Me. Lose your life of selfishness so that you can find eternal life with Me. Turn from all sin that binds you and sweetly surrender your will for Mine.

Seek Me throughout your day. I am the wind that blows softly across your face. You see Me in the majestic splendor of the rising and setting sun. All creation cries out that I am Creator of the universe. Lift your eyes to the hills where I dwell in My sanctuary. Pause throughout your day to praise Me from a thankful heart full of love.

Daughter, **pray** for My strength. **Pray** for My anointing. **Pray** for My favor. **Ask** for My forgiveness. I am your Father who longs to give you good gifts and have close fellowship with you. But you must walk away from the worthless and destructive ways of this earthly world. There is no loss in doing so, but tremendous gain . . . eternal life, abundant Promised Land living right here on this earth. The journey I have for you, while sometimes difficult, is also exciting and full of rich rewards.

Partake in the fruit of My Spirit. Walk on My path of Truth and do not be led astray. I am the Lord your God. I am faithful!

Forever yours,

Your loving Father

"*For* whoever wants to save his life will lose it,
but whoever loses his life for me will find it.
What good will it be for a man if he gains the
whole world, yet forfeits his soul? Or what can
a man give in exchange for his soul? For the
Son of Man is going to come in his Father's
glory with his angels, and then he will
reward each person according to
what he has done."
Matthew 16:25-27

"*If* you, then, though you are evil, know how to
give good gifts to your children, how much more
will your Father in heaven give good gifts
to those who ask him!"
Matthew 7:11

But the fruit of the Spirit is love, joy, peace,
patience, kindness, goodness, faithfulness,
gentleness and self-control.
Galatians 5:22

Pause and Ponder

As the sunset kisses you goodnight, remember all of God's love gifts throughout your day and give thanks. Rest peacefully in His arms of love and remember the wondrous things He has done for you.

From My Heart to Yours

My Heavenly Father, thank you for today's gifts and new mercies. I am grateful for these opportunities and blessings You brought my way:

_____

_____

_____

_____

_____

_____

_____

_____

_____

_____

_____

_____

_____

_____

_____

_____

_____

_____

_____

Pruned to Bear Fruit

*D*aughter, I am pruning you in the sweet, flowery garden of your life. I am cutting back branches that bear no fruit, weeding out thoughts and attitudes that threaten to choke out the beauty of the blooms within your heart. Like a butterfly in metamorphosis, I am transforming you into all I have created you to be so you can sprout wings of utter beauty and fly.

Savor each day as it comes. Look for, and learn from, each day's lessons. The possibilities of a life well-honed in the fiery furnace of sacrifice and adversity are endless. Open the eyes of your heart, look through the lens of heaven, and see as I see. Beauty to behold will unfold as I snip away the wilted leaves on your branches.

Live each day wrapped in the glory meant for that one day. Hold tightly to My hand and be full of My joy as I lead you along the path carefully chosen just for you. Keep the gate to your garden closed off to the enemy and all of his tactics, being careful not to open even the slightest crack. One tiny seed of destruction will spread disease like wildfire throughout your garden, killing off the lovely blooms I tenderly cultivate.

Be on guard, celebrate each day with praise, glorify My name, and live a life of love. My peace and My joy I give to you abundantly. Go forth in power today. Spread your wings of color and FLY!

Bloom beautifully,

Your loving Father

He cuts off every branch in me that bears no fruit, while every branch that does bear fruit he prunes so that it will be even more fruitful.
John 15:2

Your boasting is not good. Don't you know that a little yeast works through the whole batch of dough?
1 Corinthians 5:6

But as for me, I will always have hope; I will praise you more and more. My mouth will tell of your righteousness, of your salvation all day long, though I know not its measure.
Psalm 71:14-15

Pause and Ponder

When we plant our lives in God's perfect, unfailing love, we can grow and flourish beyond anything imaginable.

From My Heart to Yours

Father, today I choose to see the world as You see it. What lessons have I learned from trusting You? How can I help others learn to trust You?

_____

_____

_____

_____

_____

_____

_____

_____

_____

_____

_____

_____

_____

_____

_____

_____

_____

_____

_____

_____

_____

Whispers

Expect a Miracle Today

In the stillness of the morning, I call your name. I beckon you into My presence for sweet fellowship that strengthens your soul. Pursue Me with the eagerness of a child opening a package with the promise of a treasure inside waiting to be revealed.

My child, greet Me each morning with a heart that cries out My name in anticipation of the miracles I have waiting for you.

Open your arms wide to receive My grace that is sufficient for every trial or temptation that comes your way. Embrace My mercy freely given to you. As you forgive those who wronged or offended you on life's journey, I also forgive all your trespasses, casting them as far as the east is from the west to be remembered no more.

My peace I give unto you as you trust Me with each decision, care, and thought. My love will light your face aglow as you are filled and refilled as you pray continually and give thanks for the gift of life you've been given today. Joy and contentment will be your closest companions when you put the interest of others ahead of your own.

This is a day that I have made—rejoice, be glad, embrace, and celebrate in it to the glory of the One who loves you forever.

The Miracle Maker,

Your loving Father

Glory in his holy name; let the hearts of those who seek the Lord rejoice. Look to the Lord and his strength; seek his face always. Remember the wonders he has done, his miracles, and the judgments he pronounced.
Psalm 105:3-5

Be joyful always; pray continually; give thanks in all circumstances, for this is God's will for you in Christ Jesus.
1 Thessalonians 5:16-18

Do nothing out of selfish ambition or vain conceit, but in humility consider others better than yourselves. Each of you should look not only to your own interests, but also to the interests of others. Your attitude should be the same as that of Christ Jesus.
Philippians 2:3-5

Pause and Ponder

May the window of your life be open wide to unlimited possibilities as you learn from your past mistakes and failures. The wonder of the next miracle is in front of you if you will just open your eyes and see. Discover a fresh supply of God's grace in the rising dawn of this new day abundant with limitless possibilities.

From My Heart to Yours

Father, I am excited and anticipate great things and opportunities today! I will walk in forgiveness and receive Your mercy as I believe You for:

_____

_____

_____

_____

_____

_____

_____

_____

_____

_____

_____

_____

_____

_____

_____

_____

Messenger of Love

People need hope. People need to know the overcoming power of My love. I have prepared and positioned you as My messenger to help people believe again, dream again, and find peace and rest in Me.

Remain faithful to Me as you travel along this winding road. Impart to others what I am teaching you. Whenever I stretch you, test your patience, or challenge you to overcome disappointment and setbacks, all of these lessons and experiences (when shared with others) build up the body of Christ. Just as you once lost your way, so many others are meandering mindlessly each day with no purpose. Hearts fail for lack of vision and purpose.

My message of love will ignite the purpose and passion I've planted inside of those you connect with. Tell your story. Share what I've done in and through you. Be who I've created you to be!

My anointing for you is special, just for you. Love the people, follow My leading, keep believing for the impossible, and you will arrive at your mountaintop. Along the way, your testimony will light a fire in others who will one day join you at the top in eternity. Listen closely and believe.

Relentless in My love,

Your loving Father

May the God of hope fill you with all joy and peace as you trust in him, so that you may overflow with hope by the power of the Holy Spirit.
Romans 15:13

Where there is no vision, the people perish: but he that keepeth the law, happy is he.
Proverbs 29:18 KJV

Be imitators of God, therefore, as dearly loved children and live a life of love, just as Christ loved us and gave himself up for us as a fragrant offering and sacrifice to God.
Ephesians 5:1-2

Pause and Pray

Heavenly Father, help me to love as You love—without limits, full of compassion and endless mercy. As Your witness, I am the fragrance of life in Christ Jesus and the aroma of Christ among those who are being saved and those who are perishing. Help me be Your hands, Your feet, and Your voice today.

From My Heart to Yours

How can I be the hands and feet of Christ today? How can
my presence be a blessing and lift the burdens of others?

_____

_____

_____

_____

_____

_____

_____

_____

_____

_____

_____

_____

_____

_____

_____

_____

_____

_____

_____

_____

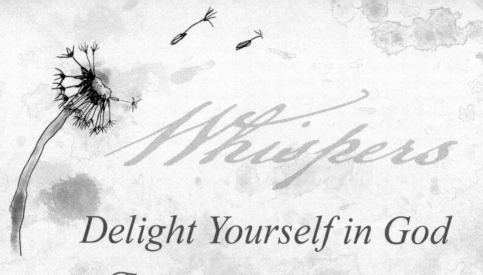

Delight Yourself in God

*F*ollow your heart, child. Follow the path that leads you to Me. Open your eyes and ears to the heart song of My creation that beckons you to draw closer to your Creator.

Delight yourself with the seemingly simple things around you. In doing so, you will find great pleasure and joy as you realize that I am fully present in your life and My love will control your response to **all** things. As the cares of this world fade to a distant drumbeat, the melodic encore of My love will call out to you, inviting you into My presence.

And it is there you will find a splendid refreshing of My strength and power. As I bathe you warmly in My love, power and strength will seep into the very depths of your being.

As you lose your will to Mine, I will raise you up as a mighty and bold witness for Me. You will walk in confidence, power, and My anointing. You will see the world through My eyes, you will hear the cries I hear, and you will recognize the broken drowning in their sea of pain.

Open yourself to Me as the cheerful flower spreads its petals to the early morning rays. Welcome Me into every part of your life for I am satisfied with nothing but your total surrender.

My grace is sufficient for you this day and is an unending supply for your growth in Me. Yield yourself to My call on your life and you will bear much fruit as you connect to Me, the life source of your everything.

Spread your wings and soar with Me to new heights. Fly on My wings of righteousness and blaze a path for others to follow. Should you stumble, I will catch you. Let My love and joy pour forth from you like rivers of living, refreshing water on all who are near you. I am with you always.

The Heartbeat of your soul,

Your loving Father

Delight yourself in the Lord and he will give you the desires of your heart.
Psalm 37:4

As for you, the anointing you received from him remains in you, and you do not need anyone to teach you. But as his anointing teaches you about all things and as that anointing is real, not counterfeit—just as it has taught you, remain in him.
1 John 2:27

"But He said, 'My grace is sufficient for you, for my power is made perfect in weakness."
1 Corinthians 12:9

Pause and Pray

Heavenly Father, my heart's delight is in drawing near to You and knowing the truth of Your Word. May the cry of my heart always be Your will and not mine, and may I bring glory to Your name in all that I do. You are the true treasure that I seek and I love You with all of my heart.

From My Heart to Yours

Lord, today I will seek You and find You in the smallest of details. I am thankful that You showed Yourself strong in these moments of my day:

_____

_____

_____

_____

_____

_____

_____

_____

_____

_____

_____

_____

Whispers

Tune in to God

My child, listen closely today for My voice. I am training you to hear Me above the busy clamor of your day. Demands fly at you from every direction making it easy to be overwhelmed and frustrated. But even in the midst of the commotion, My peace will calm your soul as you make Me the center of your universe.

I desire communion with you in all aspects of your life—not only in times of trouble. Take time throughout your day to fellowship with Me. Recognize My love gifts and purpose to give thanks continually.

I transform you by renewing your mind. Sacrifice your desires for My desires. I am molding and shaping you into a lovely vessel from which My love, My hope, and My joy will overflow in abundance.

Tune in to Me as I equip you to move forward in all I have called you to do. Go forth with power today and walk in the confidence I have placed in you through My Son, Jesus.

Ever onward in confidence,

Your loving Father

For in him we live and move and have our being.
As some of your own poets have said,
'We are his offspring.'
Acts 17:28

"My sheep listen to my voice; I know them, and
they follow me. I give them eternal life, and they
shall never perish; no one can snatch
them out of my hand."
John 10:27-28

Be joyful always, pray continually; give thanks
in all circumstances, for this is God's will
for you in Christ Jesus.
1 Thessalonians 5:16-18

Pause and Pray

Father, I praise Your holy name! How my heart rejoices that Your peace floods my soul no matter what chaos swirls around me. I am ever thankful for Your presence that is with me wherever I go. You are awesome and mighty!

From My Heart to Yours

How can I make time in my day to commune with the Father? How can I take practical steps toward walking in more confidence through Him?

_____

_____

_____

_____

_____

_____

_____

_____

_____

_____

_____

_____

_____

_____

_____

_____

_____

_____

_____

_____

_____

_____

_____

_____

Are You Ready?

*Y*ou say you are ready, daughter, but are you? Your heart longs to break free and run on the path I've laid before you, but are you really ready?

Throughout my Word are stories of those who followed Me and accomplished great things in My name, but their task was difficult. Their choices often heartrending. Easy was not on their horizon.

When you pick up your cross and follow Me, sacrifice is inevitable. It is a required act of obedience but one that brings forth much joy. Even though the road you travel will be filled with sink holes and bumps, the final destination into eternity with Me is a rapturous existence full of My inexpressible glory.

Be brave and courageously take your stand. You know all that I've placed in your heart. Your desires line up with Mine. These next steps of faith require you to completely let go of all your human reasoning and expectations. As you move forward, it will be one faith step at a time. No looking back, no second-guessing, no complaining.

If you want to grab hold of the dreams and desires I have planted in your heart, then meet Me each day with joy as your strength, faith that moves mountains, and a resolve that refuses to quit.

Now, I ask again, daughter . . . are you ready? The meek will inherit My Kingdom.

Run fearlessly,

Your loving Father

Therefore, since we are surrounded by such a great cloud of witnesses, let us throw off everything that hinders and the sin that so easily entangles, and let us run with perseverance the race marked out for us.
Hebrews 12:1

Be on your guard; stand firm in the faith; be men of courage; be strong. Do everything in love.
1 Corinthians 16:13

Trust in the LORD and do good; dwell in the land and enjoy safe pasture. Delight yourself in the LORD and he will give you the desires of your heart.
Psalm 37:3-4

Pause and Ponder

Be committed to what could be rather than what is. Let the images of your dreams light up a movie in your mind and fuel your passion to see beyond what is to what can be. Open the window of your life to the limitless possibilities with God! Step out in faith, swing big, and give all you've got for the glory of God!

From My Heart to Yours

What is God speaking to your heart?
What is He resurrecting in you today?

_____
_____
_____
_____
_____
_____
_____
_____
_____
_____
_____
_____
_____
_____
_____
_____
_____
_____

Closing Thoughts from the Author

Friends,

What do the sentences of your life story reveal? God is the author of your life. Don't put a period where He puts a comma. It's okay if your beginning wasn't the perfect start you wanted. There are new chapters God will help you write! Turn your heart over to God and watch the new pages of your life unfold into an amazing story of God's redemptive glory, climaxing with wonder into a grand finale with the final period.

There is nothing more rewarding in life than having a close, personal relationship with Jesus. The joy in your heart, the wisdom that guides your every step, the strength in your weakness, and the faithfulness of God standing beside you in every trial is beyond anything this world has to offer. Wherever you are along life's journey, if you desire to draw closer to God or have never given your heart to Jesus, I encourage you to pray this prayer and receive all you need to walk each day in freedom, power, and love. An amazing life on this earth and in heaven to come awaits you with open arms. It is only one prayer away:

> "Jesus, I need you in my life. I come before You in total surrender repenting of all my sins. Oh Lord, please forgive me. I believe in my heart that You died on the cross and rose triumphant from the grave. Your blood cleanses me from all unrighteousness. Today, I receive You as my personal Lord and Savior. I confess You as Lord of my life, and I give my all to You. Thank you for saving me and making me new in You. Amen!"

Come, join me, and together let's make a difference in this world by radiating the love of God in our sphere of influence. May you choose to walk in His love every day and be someone's blessing along the way.

Forever in Him,

Brenda

Acknowledgments

First and foremost, I am thankful to God for His everlasting love that faithfully holds me close through every season of life. The Lord took me on an incredible journey of healing while writing *Whispers* and touched my life in such a deep, profound way with this project that I'll never be the same. The glory is all His. I am simply the willing vessel who penned words He knew would water my thirsty soul as well as the lives of those who will read a copy of this devotional.

I love how God strategically placed all of the right people in my path to mentor, guide, and help me throughout the making of this book. The imprint of their hearts are interwoven with mine on every page. My heart is overflowing with love and gratitude for each one of you.

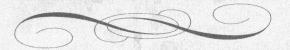

My children, Christopher, Brooke and Kyle – Your love and support gave wings to my dreams. Thank you for nudging me out of my comfort zone and seeing the bigger picture of this project.

My mother, Aileen, and sister, Melanie – my two treasured gems! Whenever I needed a listening ear, word of encouragement, or swift reality check, your arms were open for me to run into.

Dr. Charles Warren – thank you, Dad, for always being there for me. Your insightful wisdom and theological editorial help is priceless. You will forever be this little girl's hero.

My mother-in-law, Beryl Powell – Thank you for sharing your heart and faith with me and for faithfully speaking life into my God-given dreams and vision. Your unwavering support, encouragement, and love lifted me higher than you'll ever know.

Ronei Moroney – my brilliant editor and friend. You caught my heart and vision for this devotional from the beginning. Your kindness and support always encouraged me when I needed it most. We certainly shared many tears and laughs along the way. Many thanks for your superb editorial expertise in making this book a finer read. And great job writing the word prompts for the *Whispers*. Well done!

Stacey Cole –You are simply amazing. Your input, proofreading, and insight helped give birth to this book. Thank you for keeping me straight as only you can. You have the patience of Job!

Barbara – Your gift and talent as an illustrator and artist is truly amazing. You see inside my head and heart; you truly **get** me. You're not just the illustrator for all of my books but also my forever friend. Thank you for putting up with me. God put us together for a reason.

LaVerne – Thank you for tirelessly coming alongside me throughout my Whispers and writing journey. You are one of the sweetest blessings from heaven that I treasure deeply.

Lynne F. Scott – My faithful prayer warrior, author and friend who knows me inside out. Thank you for not seeing who I was, but what I could become. Your impact on my life is immeasurable.

Jennifer, Angie, Ann, Tammee, Lena, Christy, Gail, Cynthia, Brian, Hope, Randle – my blessings who shower me with endless encouragement to keep pressing on no matter what.

Rachel, Ashley, Sherry – Your love and talent elevate all that I do. Thank you for being part of my team. You are the best!

MEET THE AUTHOR
Brenda W. Powell

Brenda is a mom to three grown children and Nana to four grandchildren, with another little blessing on the way! She is the author of the new series of children's books, *The Adventures of Sugarman the Pony,* and much of her inspiration for writing comes from her beloved little grand-angels. Since launching the *Sugarman* series, Brenda has been invited to speak at multiple churches, schools, and on radio and TV shows, including Absolutely Alabama with Fred Hunter, and Trinity Broadcasting Network's Praise the Lord.

To those who know her best, Brenda lights up with the love of Jesus, is dedicated to her family, enjoys the great outdoors, loves baking and sharing her delicious cookies, and sipping a hot cup of coffee.

CONNECT WITH BRENDA:

Website: If you enjoyed *Whispers from His Heart,* check out additional products and Brenda's children's books at www.brendawpowell.com.

Blog: www.brendawpowell.com
Facebook: www.facebook.com/brenda.w.powell.7, *Sugarman the Pony*, and Author, Brenda W. Powell
Twitter: @bpowell_brenda
Instagram: brendawpowell

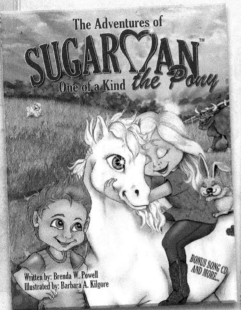
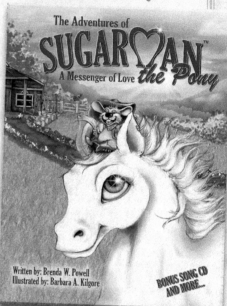

Inspire and Encourage
others with art that ministers

May my feet
outrun MY *thoughts*
MAY MY hands
out give MY **heart**
May my eyes
outsee TODAY'S **possibilities**
MAY MY dreams
overtake MY *past mistakes*

Brenda W. Powell

I can do all things through Christ who strengthens me. Phil. 4:13

8x10 canvas art print

Available for purchase at
www.brendawpowell.com

If you loved *Whispers from His Heart*, you'll enjoy Brenda's music and audio CD, **All That I Am.**

Now you can enjoy listening to Brenda's music and audio reading of several of the *Whispers* and other inspiring scriptures in your home, car, or headphones.

All That I Am, written and composed by Brenda, features contributing writer and beautiful vocals by Ashley Smith. This inspirational CD pairs anointed worship lyrics with rich notes bringing you into the presence of the Lord. Peace and tranquility set the tone as Brenda narrates some of her *Whispers* along with other uplifting scriptures to more of Brenda's soothing God-breathed and inspired background music. It's a beautiful acoustic experience you're sure to love that will encourage and give you hope. Makes a perfect gift.

Tracks include "All That I Am," Narrated Whispers: "Experiencing Joy Untold," "Arise Courageous and Bold," "His Precious Treasure," "Grace for Supernatural Peace," "Heart Song of Praise," "Receive A Standing Ovation," and "Uplifting Scriptures of Hope & Encouragement."

Purchase at www.brendawpowell.com, Amazon, CDBABY, and iTunes

Always remember and purpose to dance through life, keeping your eyes on Him, and your heart overflowing with love and thankfulness. Then you won't be able to stop that extra bounce in your step . . . and, you just might find yourself twirling.

CPSIA information can be obtained
at www.ICGtesting.com
Printed in the USA
FSHW01n0003200918
52167FS